MW00945766

STRUGGLING
WITH
GOD

A Theology for Real Life

SAM SUMNER

WestBow
PRESS®
A DIVISION OF THOMAS NELSON
& ZONDERVAN

WestBow Press books may be ordered through booksellers or by contacting:

WestBow Press
A Division of Thomas Nelson & Zondervan
1663 Liberty Drive
Bloomington, IN 47403
www.westbowpress.com
1 (866) 928-1240

ISBN: 978-1-9736-9125-9 (sc)
ISBN: 978-1-9736-9124-2 (hc)
ISBN: 978-1-9736-9126-6 (e)

Library of Congress Control Number: 2020909162

Print information available on the last page.

WestBow Press rev. date: 6/22/2020

ENDORSEMENT

Thank you Pastor Sam for a book that doesn't play it safe on tough subjects and taboo issues that many Christian books avoid. There are no pad answers in this book. It's a concise, straightforward response to the real issues of life. If you're a seeker or a seasoned believer, this will be one of the books in your library you'll constantly go back to in your efforts to more deeply know and understand God and His Word.

Ferrell Hardison,
Pastor, Pike's Crossroads Church

To my wife Brooks,
Your faith and passion challenge me
And make me a better husband, father, and minister.

Special thanks to Ashley Keffer

CONTENTS

FOREWORD

Finally, a theology book everyone can understand and relate to. The title alone speaks volumes. Let's be honest. Most all of us have struggled with God. And we want to believe theology does relate to real life. We are indebted to author, Sam Sumner for the transparency with which he writes. His honesty about his own personal struggles as a Christian is an encouragement to the rest of us. His writing style is also a refreshing approach, especially in a book that deals with such deep themes as the Trinity, the struggle between good and evil, the redemptive story, the deity of Christ and even the Holy Spirit. Everyone loves a story. Sam not only tells gripping stories from his own life experiences but also from the Bible. This book is both inspiring and informative. More than another theology book, more than a text book, "Struggling with God" will prove to be a handbook for life.

Randy Carter
Superintendent, Pentecostal Free Will Baptist

HOW TO READ THIS BOOK

My hope is you will not only learn more about God and the Christian life as you read through this book, but you will also engage with God personally and grow as a Christian as you progress through it. Here are a few tips to help you get the most out of your study.

First, begin and end each chapter in prayer. Ask the Holy Spirit to give you wisdom and to guide your study. In addition, pray that you will be humbled and receptive to God's Word and His truths. As you complete each chapter take note of some of the difficult truths or questions you had and take them to God. It may be you have to do this on numerous occasions but keep at it and stay humble as you wrestle out these truths with Him.

Next, when you come across something that is difficult to understand or accept take some time to worship the LORD. The LORD was clear when he stated through the prophet Isaiah, "My thoughts are not your thoughts, nor are my ways your ways…For as the heavens are higher than the earth so are my ways higher than your ways."[1] Again, the Psalmist wrote, "Such knowledge is too wonderful for me; it is high, I cannot attain it."[2] While somethings will become clearer with study and time, others may remain a mystery. For those things, we must simply stand in awe

---

[1] Isaiah 55:8–9
[2] Psalm 139:6

of who our God is and accept the limitations of our finite minds to fully grasp Him.

Lastly, you will notice I attempted to specifically reference any Scriptures I used. I suggest you read this book with your Bible and read the Scriptures in context from an accurate and readable translation. The Christian should make it a habit to examine everything in the light of Scripture. Some suggested translations you could use include NASB, NKJV, ESV, NIV, or NLT. Getting into the rhythm of reading the Bible on a daily basis and not just trusting what others have to say about it is one of the ways to make your faith your own.

INTRODUCTION

It was fall semester, 1998. I was sitting in Dr. Zervos's New Testament Greek class. I decided to take the course because I recently accepted the call to preach and thought learning more about the language of the New Testament would be beneficial. Initially, I was excited because I had seen how some preachers used the Greek to more fully explain the Bible, and I just knew that a new world was about to open up to me. Was it ever! I had no idea what I was in for.

I realized pretty quickly I was way in over my head. The only thing that made me feel any better was a frat guy who came in about every day with a deer in the headlights look. Almost every time he was asked a question he would say, "I have no idea...the only reason I'm in here is because I couldn't find another elective." He would then go on about how he had partied way too much the night before to be able to get into this. Eventually, he actually got into it, as did I. Mostly because we had a pretty awesome professor.

However, over the next few weeks I found myself sitting in class filled with all kinds of emotions. Part of me was ticked off, while the other part was heartbroken, and yet another part of me was intrigued. You see, I had been raised in church and taught for as long as I can remember that the Bible was the Word of God. Honestly, I had never given any deep thought as to how we got the Bible, nor had it even entered my mind to question the Bible's implicit authority. Suddenly, here I was, introduced to Biblical criticism, critical scholars, and obvious inconsistencies in the Bible I had never noticed before.

There were a couple of reasons this so difficult for me. First, the man I probably admired most in my life, my grandfather, was an old school Pentecostal preacher and he had built his life on the Bible being the infallible "Word of God." In my most honest moments, I really began to think less of him and others who took the Bible so seriously. They had lived their whole lives striving to be faithful to this book, and here I was discovering it wasn't unlike any other ancient book put together by a bunch of flawed people with agendas. In addition, it had gone through an, at best, precarious process of transmission. Finally, I was discovering that it was filled with seeming contradictions that had never really caught my attention, but there they were bright as day now.

The second reason this was a difficult struggle, was that I had a recent experience with God that totally changed my life. From about age fifteen till around nineteen I did the typical rebellious teenager thing and felt justified in doing so. In high school my kidney's failed and I had to go on dialysis, and this, after being a "faithful Christian." I felt betrayed by God and ready to indulge in everything I was missing out on.

In my second year of college, however, when my mind was on wild parties and girls, God surprisingly brought about revival in our area and many young people committed their lives to Jesus. My experience was a little different than most. Rather than walk down to the altar, I was guilted into praying for a lady who was dying with cancer. In my attempt to fulfill that promise, I got up on top of a barn where I would usually go to be by myself. As I began to pray, it felt awkward, and I felt wholly unworthy to even speak to God. As conviction gripped my heart, I could not do anything but ask for God's forgiveness. Totally caught off guard by God's grace, I was filled with new desires as I recommitted my life to Christ. Several friends and I began giving our testimonies and sharing from God's Word when we had the opportunity. God was so real to us, but what I was learning in my college classes called into question the validity of all those experiences.

Being a glutton for punishment, and an having an interest in the truth, caused me to continue taking Biblical and religious courses throughout college, few of which were favorable to Christianity or the Bible. More and more questions were raised such as the obvious question: *With all the other religions in the world, how could Christianity make the claim that it is the one true faith?* Other questions also mounted, which included the historical reliability of the Bible and trustworthiness of those who supposedly wrote it. I thought, "Could people really be so ignorant and arrogant as to dismiss all other claims to religious truth? How could people blindly accept the implicit claims of a book that was thousands of years old?" These are just a few examples, but other challenging questions were also raised.

It was a difficult and dark period for me, but I began to read, research, and pray. Ultimately, that crisis of faith brought me closer to God, caused me to dig deeper into my faith, and I came to more fully understand what I believed. During that excruciating process, my faith became my own personal possession, rather than something simply passed down to me by my family and my upbringing. My struggle had made Jesus more real to me. I came to better understand Him and His impact upon my life. I also began to appreciate Christianity's rich history and how Jesus completely changes everything.

Today, I continue to wrestle and many times, I fail, as I seek to live out my faith in real life. Things like, the Lordship of Jesus Christ, suffering, tragedy, submission, consistent prayer, self-denial, growth in righteousness, and forgiveness present great challenges. However, it is a tremendous comfort knowing that God is present with me as I struggle, and He is firmly committed until Christ is formed in me.

1

Struggling with God

For you have struggled with God and with men,
and have prevailed. —Genesis 32:28

He was not built for this. His smooth hands clutched his cloak as he attempted to slowly lay his head on the cold stone. Rarely had he slept under the stars. No sooner than he drifted off to sleep did he wake up, startled and trembling because of what he had just experienced. The sky lit up and angels went up and down on what seemed like a stairway, and it was as if the heavens opened up and something other worldly poured into his soul. Even now he couldn't find it within himself to lift his head, but he will never forget what he heard.

> I am the LORD, the God of your grandfather Abraham... The ground you are lying on belongs to you. I am giving it to your descendants. Your descendants will be as numerous as the dust of the earth... And all the families of the earth will be blessed through you.[3]

---

[3] Genesis 28:13–14

1

Sitting at his father's feet as a boy, Jacob had heard this before. It was the family blessing, but he had always assumed it would be his older brother who would receive it. After all his brother was the firstborn. However, he actually did receive the blessing from his father but not in the most honorable way.

His father, Isaac, loved Esau. He was everything you could want in a boy: manly, a faithful son, a good leader, and a great hunter. One day, Isaac calls Esau into his tent. Jacob's mother, Rebekah, knows something is up, so with a subtle glance, she gets Jacob's attention from across the yard. Jacob hurries to her side, and she tells him that the family blessing is about to go to Esau. Jacob quickly grabs his knife and sprints to the flock where he pulls out a couple of prized kids. Hurriedly, his mother uses them to make a pot of stew. She taught Esau how to cook, so she knew the exact recipe.

Jacob was about to live up to his given name. In the Hebrew language, *Jacob* means "heal snatcher," which is evidently a metaphor for a deceiver or a schemer in that culture. While his mother cooks, in the darkness of his tent Jacob's hands shake as he wraps goat skin around his arms. Isaac was blind but not stupid. Jacob knew he needed something to cover his arms because Esau was a beast of a man and felt like one, too. After completing his disguise by putting on some of Esau's clothes, he grabs the stew and heads for his father's tent.

Jacob takes a deep breath and slowly enters Isaac's tent. It seemed darker and more still than normal. So much so that Jacob actually had to call out to his father in order to find where he was. Isaac answers back, "Here I am. Who are you my son?" In sort of a whimper Jacob responds, "I am Esau, your firstborn." Suspicious, Isaacs asks, "How did you find game so quickly?" Still unable to really hold himself together Jacob says, "The Lord brought it to me." By this time, Jacob has managed to make it to his father's bedside without falling. Isaac reaches out, and his hand falls on the course goat hair on Jacob's arm. "I feel Esau, but I hear Jacob," he muses. With a cough Jacob lowers his voice, "I am Esau." With that, Jacob walks out of the tent with the patriarchal blessing and also as the object of his brother's rage.

Jacob has no choice but to flee for his life. So Rebekah sends him to live with her brother, Laban. He was only supposed to be there for a few days until Esau calmed down, but Jacob would be gone for nearly twenty years.

Here he is now, feeling lower than the dirt he attempts to find comfort in. He knows he deserves this. The schemer lied and cheated his way into being the family patriarch. Now, he flees his newly found responsibilities. He is anything but a paragon of virtue and he is certainly no example for the family he supposedly now leads. Yet, God makes a promise to Jacob, "I am with you and will keep you wherever you go, and will bring you back to this land; for I will not leave you until I have done what I have spoken to you."[4] Maybe for the first time in his life, Jacob discovers the true nature of his struggle. It's not a struggle with people or even with Esau but a struggle to get past himself, to know God on God's terms, to understand His will, and to work that knowledge and understanding into every aspect of his life.

Here's the thing. In God's promise to Jacob, He says He would be with him through that struggle. He says, "I will NOT leave you until I have done what I have spoken to you."[5] Some two thousand years later, the Apostle Paul will echo this same sentiment when he writes, "Being confident of this very thing, that He [Jesus] who has begun a good work in your will complete it until the day of Jesus Christ."[6] Jacob now has a promise from God, but his struggles are far from over.

Almost as soon as Jacob arrives in Haran, he falls in love. With elegance, Rachel approaches the well where Jacob is attempting

---

[4] Genesis 28:15

[5] Ibid.

[6] Philippians 1:6

3

to refresh himself, and he can't take his eyes off her. She was Uncle Laban's daughter, which, in that day, made a relationship between the two all the better. Since Jacob is essentially broke, he agrees to serve Laban for seven years in order to gain Rachel's hand in marriage. However, after seven years and evidently a wild wedding party, Jacob wakes up to Leah, Rachel's sister. Laban had tricked the trickster and after the fact, informed Jacob that since Leah was the eldest, the only "right" thing to do would be to see her married first. But, being ever so gracious, Laban agrees to let Jacob marry Rachel if he serves another seven years. Jacob agrees and after seven years marries Rachel also. The children from these sisters and their hand maidens would eventually make up the twelve tribes of Israel—the patriarchs of the Jewish nation.

After a few more years of service, God has been good to Jacob, and he decides it is time to leave Laban and return home— something he would not do without controversy. Jacob had become very prosperous and Laban very envious. Laban did everything he could to prevent Jacob from leaving because he knew that Jacob had brought him a large amount of wealth. However, Jacob knew his place and despite Laban's attempts to dissuade him, Jacob returned home, although not without some hesitation.

On his way, Jacob does something he has never done up to this point in his life: he addresses God by His name, "Yahweh." He prays,

> O God of my father Abraham and God of my father Isaac, *the LORD [Yahweh]* who said to me, "Return to your country and to your family, and I will deal well with you": I am not worthy of the least of all the mercies and of all the truth which You have shown Your servant; for I crossed over

this Jordan with my staff, and now I have become two companies. Deliver me.[7]

What a truly humble prayer! Jacob had left home with nothing but a staff, he had lied to his dying father, enraged his brother, and was himself the victim of chicanery. Now, he returns a very rich man with a large family and years of difficult lessons learned. Through all his struggles, Jacob was not quite the same man he was twenty years ago. The difficulties and conflicts of the preceding years had genuinely changed Jacob. Without realizing it, his struggles had not only been with Esau and Laban but with God. He had gone from a man determined to do things his way to a man utterly dependent upon God, a man vaguely aware of God's will to a man who knows full well what God has laid out for him, and a man who only heard stories about God to a man who calls God by name. Through all his struggles, God has been there, just as He had promised. He was drawing Jacob to Himself, revealing to Jacob His character, lavishing upon Jacob His love, and reminding Jacob of His will.

At this point, Jacob sits alone in dark, and what happened next is a bit of a mystery. The Bible says, "Then, Jacob was left alone; and a Man wrestled with him."[8] This was an intense struggle for they wrestled until the morning, and by the end, Jacob's hip was out of joint, yet he persisted. At some point during the fight, Jacob must have realized this was more than a mere man. In fact, Jacob would name the place "Peniel" saying he had seen the face of God. As the man attempts to leave, Jacob refuses to let go, saying, "I will not let You go unless You bless me." The man asks, "What is your name?" "Jacob," he responds. The man then states, "Your name shall no longer be called Jacob, but Israel; for you have struggled with God and with men, and have prevailed."[9]

---

[7] Genesis 32:9–10; *italics mine*

[8] Genesis 32:24

[9] Genesis 32:28

Learning from Jacob's Struggle

There are a few things that come out of this event worth noting. First, Jacob had been struggling his whole life attempting to do things his way. Because of his grandfather and father, he knew the truths of God. He had heard the stories of how God called his grandfather out of his homeland and how Abraham believed God's promise for an heir. Numerous times he had heard Isaac recount the time he and his father had walked up Mount Moriah not to offer a lamb but Isaac as the sacrifice. Isaac had told his sons what God had told his father, "I will make you a great nation; I will bless you and make your name great; and you shall be a blessing."[10] However, those truths had to be wrestled out of *Jacob's* life. Yahweh had to become *Jacob's* God, not just his grandfather's or father's God. Jacob knew he would carry on the family heritage and he must have struggled with that knowledge because it included laying aside his plans. It meant submitting to the will of Yahweh rather than forging his own path.

Truly discovering who God is and what God expects from us is very much a struggle because it is much easier to create a god of our own liking, one that is more amenable to us, one that is more docile and less demanding, rather than see Him exactly for who He is and try with everything to submit to His will as an act of worship.

Next, Jacob had to come to grips with the truth about himself. We live in a day where evil is external or just a matter of perspective. Deep down everyone is good; they just need the right environment to cultivate that goodness. The bad that occurs in the world is a result of a poor environment: a bad home life, poor education, neglect, etc. Evil is, therefore, excused or justified: the thief grew up poor, the gangbanger didn't have a father figure, the rapist was abused, the poor had no opportunity, and so on.

---

[10] Genesis 12:2

While there is some truth here, the Bible ultimately lays the blame somewhere else, making statements like, "The heart is deceitful...and desperately wicked."[11] Furthermore, it plainly states, "[T]here is none who does good . . . in sin my mother conceived me."[12] Jacob had to discover the truth about himself. He was not a truly good person who was failed by his parents. He was, at his core, a wicked schemer. When asked, "What is your name," Jacob responded honestly, "My name is Jacob [I'm the schemer]." Again, this is not an easy truth to accept and many in our world will outright reject this notion but one cannot fully understand the truths of God, grasp His will, nor fully understand our need for Him apart from this key truth: we are forever marred by sin and there is nothing we can do to change who we really are.

Finally, the man says, "You have struggled with God and have prevailed." Obviously the "win" for Jacob was not that he had defeated God, for all God had to do to end the fight was simply touch Jacob's thigh and the fight was over. This small incident clearly showed that God was in control of the entire encounter from start to finish. In his struggle, Jacob humbled himself and realized how much he needed God for he says, "I will not let go unless you bless me." Jacob had come to more fully know God and become more submissive to His will. God often allows His children to struggle, which may include letting go of those things we once trusted in, like material possession, health, other people, wealth, a fulfilling job, or even one's own family.

In addition, because of our sinful human nature, it is difficult to get past ourselves and our preconceptions about God in order to see Him for who He really is (as the Scripture reveals Him) and embrace what He expects from our lives. It's just easier to go with what seems right to us or whatever makes us most comfortable. Moreover, as we discover these truths, we also discover that they

---

[11] Jeremiah 17:9

[12] Romans 3:12; Psalm 51:5

impact or should impact our daily lives in very profound ways, and sometimes that is not an easy thing to accept. Living life by your own rules, going after whatever feels good, and looking to things or people to bring fulfillment are not easy habits to break. In fact, many times they are part of who we are. Jacob was known for persistently pursuing what he wanted until it was his. However, God patiently allows us to discover the futility of these things while saying to us, "I am with you . . . for I will not leave you until I have done what I have spoken to you."[13]

Oswald Chambers once wrote, "Faith must be tested, because it can be turned into a personal possession only through conflict."[14] *You cannot come to know God, humble yourself to accept His will, nor appreciate and adore His plan of salvation without struggle.* Just like all of us Jacob had to come to grips with the revealed truth about God (His holiness, His justice, His love, His plan) and about himself (his inability to measure up, his selfishness, his manipulative character, his SIN) and then wrestle those truths out in practical ways in his daily life as he attempts to orient himself. He experienced a Divine wounding that forever changed him. God's persistent presence in Jacob's life wore Jacob down. God allowed him to flounder, allowed him to question, allowed him to pursue frivolous things, and at times, allowed him to live life as if he were the master of his own soul. All the while God was quietly revealing Himself to Jacob and drawing Jacob closer to Himself.

A great example of this is when Jacob had finally made up his mind to return home. Notice how he contrasts Laban with God.

> Your father does not regard me with favor as he did before. *But the God of my father* has been with me . . . I have served your father with all my strength, yet your father had cheated me . . .

---

[13] Genesis 28:15

[14] Oswald Chambers. *My Upmost for His Highest* (Uhrichsville, OH: Barbour Books), August 29.

But God did not permit him to harm me. [Laban constantly changed the deal]. *Thus God* has taken away the livestock of your father and given them to me.[15]

You see what's going on here? Every challenge Jacob faced and every struggle he endured caused him to look to God and see God's person and God's activity in his life more clearly. And so, Jacob kept fighting, kept struggling reminded of the promise, "I will not leave you until I have done what I promised."[16]

Not only did Jacob's struggle with Laban bring Jacob closer to God but it also revealed the nature of God to his wives. Notice their response as they realized their father had essentially disowned them while God abundantly provided for them,

Is there any portion or inheritance left to us in our father's house? Are we not regarded by him as foreigners? For he has sold us, and he has indeed devoured our money. All the wealth that God has taken away from our father belongs to us and to our children. Now then, whatever God has said to you, do.[17]

Even though this may have been a difficult truth about their father for the women to grasp, it was true nonetheless. However, this struggle of both Jacob and his wives revealed more clearly the nature, character, and love of God who provides for them and takes them up when others would forsake them or take advantage of them.

Ultimately the events of the preceding years drastically changed Jacob and deeply affected those around him. His struggle

---

[15] Genesis 31:5–10 ESV; *italics mine*

[16] Genesis 28:15

[17] Genesis 31:14–16 ESV

with God and with man brought him closer to the God of his grandfather and father. This God is now personally known to him and Jacob has learned to trust Him and submit to His will. After his encounter with the man on the eve of his return home, Jacob would limp the rest of his days and thus have a constant reminder that his struggles, though difficult, made God more real to him, showed Jacob exactly who Jacob was, and changed him for good. He was no longer "Heal snatcher" but "Israel," which means "He struggles with God."

My Prayer for You

I pray this would not be an ordinary theology book. I believe a true and intimate knowledge of who God is comes only through a real struggle. This includes going through the time and effort to draw near to God,[18] know Him deeply, discovering His plans and purposes, and then seriously seeking to work that into your everyday life.[19]

It is in our struggles we more clearly see God and when God most dramatically changes us. The heroes of Scripture are those who engaged in that conflict and though deeply flawed, sometimes frustrated, and often questioning God, they did not quit wrestling, they persevered and found themselves with a deeper, more intimate knowledge of the God they worshiped and a clearer understanding of His will for their life.

Real theology does not happen in a vacuum but in real life and through real struggle. As we go through just a few key aspects of the Christian faith, I hope you are challenged. I hope you will allow the Holy Spirit to show you yourself in the light of Scripture. I hope you will engage God personally throughout this book. This can be more than a mere mental exercise but an

---

[18] James 4:8
[19] Philippians 2:12–16

encounter. As Christians, we see our struggles, our questions, our difficulties, and even our internal frustrations as opportunities to go to God, and though we may not find every answer and life will not always get better, we find that God is there just as he promised Jacob; "I am with you . . . for I will not leave you until I have done what I have spoken to you."[20] In his landmark book, *The Holiness of God*, R.C. Sproul wrote, "...for the transforming power of God to change our lives, we must wrestle with Him."[21] As God works in us during our struggles, He will change us into the image of Christ which is His will and ultimate end of all good theology.

---

[20] Genesis 28:15

[21] R.C. Sproul. *The Holiness of God* (Carol Stream, Ill: Tyndale House Publisher, Inc.), Kindle ed.

2

Jesus: Man, Lamb, LORD

Who are you Lord? . . . I am Jesus. —Acts 9:5

He was a very ambitious young man from a cosmopolitan city. In that city, he was exposed to different cultures and viewpoints covering numerous philosophical and theological backgrounds, and he was mentored by the one of the greatest rabbis of his time. Personally, he immersed himself in the Jewish Scriptures and the traditions, and with great pride and determination he sought to follow those things to the letter of the Law. He was proud of his Jewish heritage and Roman citizenship. As a result of his hard work Saul, in his words, "advanced in Judaism beyond many of [his] contemporaries."[22] He became a Pharisee and a part of that august Jewish body, the Sanhedrin.

A driven man, Saul did not back down when a new sect of Judaism arose claiming that some crucified criminal was, in fact, the Messiah and God in the flesh. He made it his mission to stamp out this blasphemous sect by whatever means necessary. Pleading his case Saul gained the approval of the Sanhedrin to hunt these heretics down and force them to recant or put them in prison. After consenting to the gruesome death of a young

---

[22] Galatians 1:14

man named Stephen, who was stoned because of his belief in this Messiah, Saul knew his crusade would not be an easy one, but that only fueled his zeal, and he increased his persecution of the followers of this Messiah, Jesus Christ.

As of result of intense persecution, many of the followers of Jesus were forced out of Jerusalem. However, Saul was dogged in his pursuit, and the writer of Acts tells us "Saul uttered threats with every breath and was eager to kill the Lord's followers."[23] Eventually, Saul's intense zeal would take him beyond the region of Judea, to Damascus. So zealous was Saul, he was intent on destroying the Church. However, on the way Saul would have an encounter that would forever change the course of his life.

After receiving authority from the high priest, Saul and his entourage struck out for Damascus. On the way, a light suddenly shone around Saul, and he fell to the ground. In an instant, everything Saul knew to be true, and everything he had built his life upon was dramatically challenged. A voice from heaven thundered, "Saul, Saul, why are you persecuting Me?"[24] Saul's response was short but telling; "Who are you Lord?" He knows whoever this is, He is supreme, and the answer comes back, "I am Jesus." What a shock this must have been! This was the name that Saul had grown to hate. Now, as he trembled in fear, Saul responded, "Lord, what do You want me to do?"

In an instant, this once proud Pharisee was brought low. Blinded by the encounter, Saul had to be led by the hand the rest of the way to Damascus. Alone and blinded, Saul could not help but examine everything he had come to believe, along with himself. He was certainly disturbed by what he discovered. In many ways, he felt helpless. There was nothing he could do about his sin. Everything he thought he had accomplished for God, he now knows was less than nothing. He would later come to

---

[23] Acts 9:1 NLT

[24] Acts 9:4 NLT

describe all his accomplishments as "dung." For the rest of his life, Saul would never forget the man he was before he met Jesus. Right up until the end of his life, Saul would call himself a "wretched man" and the "worst of sinners." Talk about your world being turned upside down.

As far as Jesus goes, Oh! The questions that must have rolled through his mind! *Was Jesus really the foretold Messiah? If so, how did I miss Him? Is He God or man or both . . . but no man could be God, right? Why would he subject himself to such persecution and a brutal death? I thought Messiah would usher in a Kingdom yet this man was crucified.* In addition, he may have asked, *Of all people, why would He speak to me?* Being a Pharisee and knowing the Scriptures as well as he did, Saul likely rehearsed all the Messianic promises over and over in his head. Everything Saul knew about the Scriptures would gradually begin to come into focus as he looked at them afresh through the lens of Jesus Christ. Saul would immediately find himself preaching about his conversion, but he would also face resistance.

Just as God had done with many of the Old Testament prophets, He hid Saul away in the deserts of Arabia for about three years. There, Saul likely wrestled out his theology in light of the Scriptures and his dramatic encounter with Jesus. It must not have been easy for Saul to unlearn everything he thought he knew, but the truth could not be denied. N.T. Wright suggests Saul was following the traditions of the prophets, like Elijah, by going to the desert, and in doing so, he may have been complaining, questioning himself, and seeking clarity.[25] Those questions that bombarded his thoughts during that period of blindness were worked out in great detail here, alone, in the desert, in prayer and study. It was in that desert that Saul's most profound struggle

---

[25] N.T. Right, *Paul, Arabia, and Elijah*, ntwrightpage.com, http://www.ntwrightpage.com/Wright_Paul_Arabia_Elijah.pdf (Accessed September 2017).

took place. No longer was he fighting evil by attempting to purify his religion and maintain his own personal holiness, but he was embracing a victory over evil that had already been won on a cross by a slain carpenter from Nazareth who was God incarnate. Saul died in that desert as did his attempts to save himself by piety and zeal. The man who emerged would be a man utterly dependent upon God's grace and wholly devoted to His message; God has come into the world in the person of Jesus Christ to save sinners. Eventually, Saul's name would be changed to Paul as a testament to his change in character wrought by God.

After his amazing encounter, Paul would never be the same and neither would the world. He would become the church's most zealous missionary, and he would take the message of Jesus far beyond the region of Judea. He would preach in the ancient world's largest cities, plant churches, become a pastor's pastor, and raise up leaders all over the Roman Empire, and he did it in a day when travel was tedious and treacherous and when the main form of communication was letters. His letters would eventually make up nearly two thirds of the New Testament, and his articulation of the person and work of Jesus Christ would be unmatched. By his personal encounter with Jesus and through the tutelage of the Holy Spirit, Paul would not only bring clarity to Jesus and His work but would also, like no one else, explain exactly how those truths should impact the lives of all believers.

Just like Paul, many will wrestle with the question, "Who is Jesus?" In fact, ask most anyone today and most will have an opinion on Jesus. He was a good man, a key figure in history, a great teacher, or maybe even a prophet. Every Easter and Christmas numerous documentaries claiming *new* information or original perspectives on the life of Jesus run on the *History Channel*, *NatGeo*, or *Discovery*. Of course, most of the new information is neither new nor are the perspectives original. It seems almost every year some scholar, author, religious leader, or reporter trying to make a name for themselves comes out with a controversial book about Jesus; *The Da Vinci Code* or *Zealot: The Life and Times of Jesus of Nazareth* are just a couple of examples.

Personally, I can vividly remember my disappointment in college as I heard Jesus compared to pagan deities such as Dionysus, Horus, or Mithras.[26] It seemed obvious the Gospel writers simply ripped off their stories from the ancient Greeks and other Near Eastern myths. It wasn't until after much research and study that I discovered many of the so called similarities were assumed by scholars as they attempted to translate and interpret much of the ancient material in the light of the familiar Gospel stories. For example, there is a list of similarities between Horus and Jesus anyone can find on the internet, which seem to prove the point but as scholarship has improved, it now makes these lists look outright fabricated.

The person of Jesus is not limited to the halls of higher institutions or Sunday mornings. In pop culture, Kanye West, Faith Hill, P. Diddy, & others have sung songs about Jesus, many wear T-shirts with his face on them, and in one form or another, some even thank Him for their success. In a not so subtle lampoon of many celebrities and athletes, Will Ferrell's character, in *Talladega Nights,* even prays to "baby Jesus" in his "golden fleece diapers."

With all this exposure, you would think that Jesus would be more well-known than any other historical figure. Who He was and what He came to do would be clear. However, it seems that all the attention surrounding Jesus has only clouded who He really is. Paul warned the Corinthian church that some would come preaching "another Jesus" and that is exactly what we see happening today. Looking at Paul's warning, we see the controversy surrounding Jesus is nothing new. So, who exactly is Jesus and what did he come to do? We will look at Jesus through

---

[26] Stephen Harris, editor. *Understanding the Bible*, 5th ed. (Mountain View, CA: Mayfield Publishing Company, 2000), 326-334.

three lenses to better understand who the real Jesus is and grasp what He accomplished. Please note that this is not an exhaustive Christology but more of a fly-over or introduction to the person and work of Jesus Christ. The three lenses we will look through are Man, Lamb, and Lord.

Man

Jesus grew up in a small town in northern Judea called Nazareth. This was a "redneck" area of Judea where cars were up on blocks and past times included hunting and questionable activities out in the middle of some field on the weekends. People there had a distinctive accent and were generally looked down upon by those from more refined and educated regions of Judea.

Jesus also had a questionable heritage. His mother claimed to be a virgin. "Yeah, right," surely was the attitude of many. The Jewish Talmud even suggests that Jesus was actually the illegitimate son of a Roman soldier, thus it is likely that very few people believed Mary's story that her son was the result of the overshadowing of the Holy Spirit. The assumption was that she was likely knocked up. As a result, Jesus and his family were probably shunned and his childhood would have been difficult. Humanly speaking this would have given Joseph and Mary a good reason to move down to Egypt for a while.

As a Jew, Jesus would have gone to synagogue regularly where he would have thoroughly learned what we call the Old Testament. He and his family would observe the Jewish festivals, which he would later use to teach people about Himself. In addition, Jesus came up during a time of resurgent Jewish Pride, so Messianic expectations were extremely high, and they varied from group to group. Finally, Jesus' name was a very common one. In the Hebrew, it was "Joshua," and it meant "salvation" but he might as well have been named John, Bill, or Jim. He was a common peasant from a backwater part of the Roman Empire. In Christ, God humbled Himself and as Max Lucado writes, "[He] refused to be a statue in a cathedral or a priest in an elevated pulpit, He chose instead to be Jesus."[27]

Many Christians have so deified Jesus that we tend to forget that he was a man. He laughed, wept, played with children, loved his friends, obeyed His parents, grew, and even learned new things. The book of Hebrews gives us some very interesting information about Jesus' humanity.

First, Hebrews 4:15 says he was "touched with the feeling of our infirmities," and because of that he is a sympathetic high priest that knows our struggles, weaknesses, frustrations, and difficulties. We do not serve a God who sits oblivious in the heavens completely separated from our suffering and frustrations, but One who knows very well, and even to a greater extent than we can imagine, the suffering and struggle of humanity. Isaiah called the Messiah, a "man of sorrows." Hebrews 4:15 also says that Jesus was tempted in every point as we are. So he knows what it is to resist human nature and to resist the enemy. In fact, Hebrews says He resisted it to the point of blood! Finally, Hebrews 5:8 says that Jesus "learned obedience by the things which he suffered." Luke speaks of Jesus' growth as a child. Speaking about Jesus' growth as strong statement of his humanity, A.J. Conyers makes this comment; "For the experience of human life is not one of completeness . . . but one of learning and maturing in different areas of life."[28]

Not only does Jesus identify with us in our humanity by being human in virtually every way, but as a man, Jesus makes God known. In his book, *Christian Theology*, Alister McGrath outlines the history of Christian theology and its development.

---

[27] Max Lucado. *God Came Near* (Sisters, OR: Multnomah Publishers Inc., 1986), 53.

[28] A.J. Conyers. *A Basic Christian Theology* (Nashville, TN: B&H Academic, 1995), 89.

On the subject of Jesus' humanity, he points out that historically theologians say that as man, Jesus determines life's shape, that he is the revelation of the destiny of man.[29] In other words, *Jesus is what we ought to be.* As Paul would put it, we are to be "conformed to the image of [Christ]."[30] He is our supreme example and though we will never perfectly mirror his image in this life, the Apostle John writes with great anticipation, "When he is revealed, we shall be like him."[31]

Lamb

Before Jesus, there was a disheveled wild-eyed prophet drawing a crowd from all over Judea. His message was simple, yet offensive, "Repent!" No one was excused. In his preaching the rich, the tax collectors, the soldiers, the ruling class, and even the righteous Pharisees were fodder for the fire of judgement. However, his message was not without hope. Although many felt that John was the One promised by the prophets, he was clear, "I am not the Christ . . . but He who is coming after me that is mightier than I."[32] And for all the time John spent pointing out sin, one day Jesus arrived, and John pointed to Him and declared, "Behold! The Lamb of God who takes away the sin of the world!"[33]

For us, the phrase "lamb of God" may be so familiar we don't take time to absorb its full meaning, or it may go right over our heads with no idea what John was trying to convey. To fully understand what John meant when he called Jesus the "Lamb of God," we must take a look at the Old Testament sacrificial system.

---

[29] Alister McGrath. *Christian Theology: An Introduction* (Malden, MA: Blackwell Publishing, 2001), 350.
[30] Romans 8:29
[31] 1 John 3:2
[32] Matthew 3:11
[33] John 1:29

In the Old Testament, the Tabernacle and later the Temple were vivid reminders of the separation between God and man. That separation was due to sin, both inherent sin and sins committed. Sin had to first be "covered" or "atoned" before one could approach God. The writer of Hebrews states, "Without shedding of blood there is no remission [of sin]."[34] The offering of an innocent and pure animal was a reminder that sin equals death and that God takes sin seriously. In short, the worshiper was to lay their hand upon the head of the animal, thus transferring their guilt to that innocent animal, then the animal would be killed in the place of the individual, family, or nation. That animal became a substitute.

Probably the most prominent of these sacrifices was the Passover lamb. Once a year during Passover, pilgrims from all over the region would come to Jerusalem, many bringing with them a young lamb, "without blemish," that was supposed to be raised in the home for some time prior. Likely, this lamb had become like a pet. That pet would have its neck slit and its blood poured at the base of the altar. It would taste death in the place of those who offered it. Although thousands of lambs were sacrificed at the festival, the Scripture speaks of *the* lamb singularly, as if only one lamb was to be sacrificed. Again, according to the author of Hebrews these sacrifices pointed to a much greater sacrifice, "the blood of Christ."

Just as the first sacrificial lambs offered in Egypt during the Exodus, and the thousands offered afterward to commemorate that event, Jesus' perfect sacrifice takes away the penalty of death for all those affected by sin. Paul sums it up perfectly, "For He made Him who knew no sin to be sin for us, that we might become the righteousness of God in Him."[35] Paul's summation of the sacrifice of Christ goes much further than the Old Testament sacrifices. Those sacrifices could only temporarily "cover" sin while

---

[34] Hebrews 9:22
[35] 1 Corinthians 5:21

Jesus' sacrifice cleanses from all sin, and in the eyes of God, makes one righteous or justified.

Isaiah paints a very clear picture of Messiah's work some seven hundred years before Jesus. He writes,

> Surely He has borne our griefs and carried our sorrows; Yet we esteemed Him stricken, smitten by God, and afflicted. But He was wounded for our transgressions, He was bruised for our iniquities . . . And the Lord has laid upon Him the iniquity of us all . . . He was led as a lamb to slaughter . . . Yet it pleased the Lord to crush Him. . . He shall see the labor of His soul and be satisfied.[36]

Jesus tasted death on our behalf, His sacrifice cleanses us from sin, and His perfect life makes us righteous.

LORD

In the years following the resurrection of Christ, Christianity began to spread throughout the Roman Empire. Though, not without opposition. The threats and actions of the Jews against the belief in Christ as Messiah are clearly documented in the New Testament. However, once the new faith became a threat to the peace of Rome, Christianity eventually found itself an enemy of the Roman Empire. One way in which Rome tested the loyalty of its subjects was the public recitation of the words, "Kaiser kurious" or "Caesar is lord." While Christians were generally good citizens, they refused to exalt Caesar with the title, "Lord." That title belonged to Jesus Christ alone.

Even though the term "Lord" is a title that essentially means

---

[36] Isaiah 53:4–11a

"Master," Christians from the very beginning understood this to mean that Christ was in fact, God, come in the flesh. Paul, in one of his earliest letters, quotes a short common creed when he says, "…no one can say *Jesus is Lord*' except by the Holy Spirit."[37] And, in Romans 9:5 Paul explicitly says, "Christ came, who is over all, the eternally blessed God." John's Gospel is full of direct statements about Jesus's divinity, and even in the first couple of lines, he states plainly, "…the Word [Jesus] was with God, and *the Word was God*."[38] In addition, one of the oldest surviving sermons after the close of the New Testament begins, "Brethren, *we ought to think of Jesus Christ as of God*, the judge of the living and the dead…"[39]

However, this was a truth subtly obscured in the early church where we find leaders like Arius who denied Christ's deity, demoting Him to a created being. Then, on to the scene, steps Athanasius, who refuses to allow Arius's heresy to go unchallenged. After a series of debates and exiles the *Nicene Creed* made a clear statement of the Biblical doctrine of Christ's divinity;

> We believe…in one Lord Jesus Christ, the only begotten Son of God, Begotten of the Father before all ages. Light of light, true God of true God, begotten not made, of one substance with the Father; through Him all things were made…[40]

In line with the clear teaching of the Bible, the early church fathers rightly declare Jesus Christ as the Lord.

Jesus being God in the flesh has some radical implications.

---

[37] 1 Corinthians 12:23; *italics mine*

[38] John 1:1; *italics mine*

[39] thegospelcoalition.org, *How We Can Know the New Testament Teaches that Jesus is God*; Justin Taylor, February 8, 2019.

[40] Henry Battenson & Chris Maunder, ed. *Documents of the Christian Church* (Oxford: Oxford University Press, 1999), 28.

First, it means that God can be known. Jesus is the image of the invisible God, and His descent into this world is God's way of revealing Himself to us. If you want to know what God is like or who God is, look at Jesus. Second, unable to save ourselves or obtain the righteousness required to see God, God Himself has come down to meet us where we are.[41] In doing so, He took upon Himself our sin and death and bestowed upon us His righteousness, fulfilling the types and shadows of the Old Testament. God did that!! Third, God knows the human experience. Remember, the book of Hebrews calls Him a sympathetic high priest. He's not aloof, distant, and unmoved by the human condition. Finally, if Jesus is God, He is to be worshiped and given our sole allegiance.

Addendum: King

One other item concerning Jesus's identity concerns the claim of the Gospels that He was the promised Messiah. In the Old Testament, the Messiah was also equated with a coming King who would bring the nation of Israel back to a place of glory and set the world right. The expectations for Messiah in Jesus' time were wide ranging but could be boiled down to a great leader who would deliver the Jews from the oppression of Rome and reestablish the earthly kingdom of Israel in the likeness of Israel's greatest king, David.

During Jesus' lifetime, many false Messiahs came and went. Many were ruthlessly crushed by the power of Rome which didn't take lightly any talk of rebellion or the possibility of another king besides the Roman Emperor. Thus the hopes of many Jews were dashed. So, when Jesus was crucified, how was His fate and His Kingdom different from those other so called Messiahs?

The difference lies in the nature of Jesus' Kingdom. When asked by some Pharisees when the Kingdom of God would

---

[41] Philippians 2:5–11

come, Jesus answered, "The kingdom of God does not come with observation; nor will they say, 'See here!' or 'See there!' For indeed, the kingdom of God is within you."[42] When pressed by Pilate about His Kingdom, Jesus stated, "My Kingdom is not of this world."[43]

On the surface, it seemed that Jesus failed miserably. In fact, he didn't seem to come anywhere close to satisfying the Jewish hopes for Messiah, but in reality, Jesus far surpassed their expectations. His destiny was not to rule a temporary earthly kingdom but an eternal Kingdom that was initiated in the hearts of men changed by God. It was the rule of God in the hearts and minds of men as they willingly and lovingly obey their supreme and loving King, Jesus. This is what is called the "now" aspect of the Kingdom, which is the rule of God in which God's people live out His commands in the midst of a rebellious world.

There is also the "not yet" aspect the Kingdom, in which Jesus physically returns to exact His wrath upon a rebellious planet and rule as both *God* and *King*. In that way, the Kingdom is not fully come. While the "now" aspect of the Kingdom exists alongside the world system (like a secret invasion) showing the world what one day will be, what should be, there will come a day in which Jesus suddenly arrives in all His glory to the wonder and amazement of His people and to the dread of those who have refused Him. C.S. Lewis describes it this way,

> God is going to invade alright: but what is the good of saying you're on His side then when you see the whole natural universe melting away like a dream or something else... For the first time it will be God without disguise; something so overwhelming that it will strike irresistible love

---

[42] Luke 17:20–21
[43] John 18:36

or irresistible horror into every creature. It will be too late then to choose your side. There is no use saying you choose to lie down when it has become impossible to stand up.[44]

In that day, the hope of the prophets will be fully realized and Jesus will be unveiled as the "King of Kings and the Lord of Lords," the one who has come to exact justice, bring about everlasting peace, and set the world right.

---

[44] C.S. Lewis. *Mere Christianity* (New York, NY: Touchstone, 1996), 66

3

Salvation

Most assuredly, I say to you, unless one is born again,
he cannot see the kingdom of God. —John 3:3

Nicodemus had devoted his life to keeping every aspect of the Law to include the traditions of the elders. He counted his steps on the Sabbath, was careful to observe the purity laws, attended the synagogue regularly, tithed on every last cent, and fasted every Monday and every Thursday. When he did eat, he was careful to only eat that which was kosher. The list could go on and on. Nicodemus had mastered religious duty. He had secured his place in society through his piety and devotion to the rules. He was honored with the best seats in the synagogue, and because of his clout, he was always the center of attention when he entered a room. People admired him, and as a rabbi, his teaching was sought after.

Not only did people see him as an example, but his dedication to the Law gained him God's approval, at least in the eyes of the people. His prayers carried more weight and his sacrifices were just a little more acceptable. His salvation was based upon his performance and his performance was in a word, flawless. If there were any righteous people in 1st century Judea, it was the Pharisees, and Nicodemus was more than your average Pharisee.

He was part of the Sanhedrin and a highly respected teacher of the Law. So it was no surprise that when an up and coming rabbi arrived, Nicodemus was curious.

One night they arranged to meet. Jesus cut to the chase stating, "Unless one is born again, he cannot see they kingdom of God."[45] "Wait a minute!" thinks Nicodemus, "Born again? Don't you realize how much work I've put in?" Then sarcastically Nicodemus quips, "How can a man be born when he is old? Can he enter a second time into his mother's womb and be born?"[46] You see, Nicodemus spent his life putting the right checks in the box. He had worked hard to secure his place in the kingdom, and for some upstart rabbi to suggest salvation was possibly something beyond his control (i.e. "birth") was an insult. However, Nicodemus was willing to keep listening.

The young rabbi went on to explain that salvation was a matter of faith using the illustration of Moses lifting up the serpent in the wilderness. Just as everyone had been exposed to the venomous and deadly bite of the fiery serpents, every person has been infected and corrupted by the deadly disease of sin, even Nicodemus. The only hope the people had was to look to a bronze serpent wrapped around a pole. Not one had the ability to cure themselves. Such a strange command, especially for a God who strictly forbade the forging of any graven images. Nicodemus struggles to understand. Jesus explains further that HE is the serpent and in order for anyone to be saved, they must look to Him. The image of the serpent was always associated with sin and bronze the only metal at the time that could sustain fire, the symbol of judgement. Thus the image of the bronze serpent is that of *sin judged*. That meant Jesus would taste the judgement of humanity's sin.

For Nicodemus, this meant all his hard work and devotion was for naught. His good deeds and strict obedience to the Law and

---

[45] John 3:3
[46] John 3:4

the traditions did nothing to save him or gain him God's favor. To be sure, he knew of the prophet Isaiah's declaration, "We are *all* infected and impure with sin. When we display *our righteous deeds, they are nothing but filthy rags...*"[47] However, this was a difficult truth for a man who worked so hard at being righteous to grasp. Jesus' path to salvation was too simple; "...whoever *believes* in Him should not perish but have everlasting life."[48]

While Nicodemus was asking, "What can I DO?" Jesus was essentially saying you can't DO anything. Years later the Apostle Paul would say it this way, "For by grace you have been saved through faith, and that not of yourselves; it is the gift of God, not of work, lest anyone should boast."[49] The *New Living Translation* says, "God saved you by His grace when you believed. And you cannot take credit for this; it is a gift of God."[50] The following verse makes it so there is no misunderstanding as to *how* one is saved: "Salvation is not a reward for the good things we have done, so none of us can boast about it."[51]

For his whole life, Nicodemus had, essentially, been applauded for his religious performance. It must have been very sobering for a man of his stature to accept what Jesus was saying. However, deep inside, he must have known it was true or else he wouldn't have come to Jesus with these questions. For some reason, likely God's grace, he knew all his efforts were futile. As good as Nicodemus had been, something gnawed at him, and though he struggled to accept what Jesus had to say, deep down he knew Jesus was right. "Nicodemus, you can't *do* anything." At that point, maybe, Nicodemus finally understood what David meant when he wrote in Psalms 40,

---

[47] Isaiah 64:6 NLT; *italics mine*
[48] John 3:16; *italics mine*
[49] Ephesians 2:8–9
[50] Ephesians 2:8 NLT
[51] Ibid, v. 9

If I tried to recite all your wonderful deeds, I would never come to the end of them. You take no delight in sacrifices or offerings. Now that you have made me listen, I finally understand you don't require burnt offerings or sin offerings. Then I said, "Look, I have come. As is written about me in the Scriptures: I take joy in doing your will, my God, for your instructions are written on my heart."[52]

God the Father and Jesus did not want Nicodemus' white knuckle religious obedience while his heart resisted and remained unchanged. No, the Father was not pleased with that kind of effort, no matter how noble, humanly speaking. He wanted obedience from the heart and that only came by admitting one's utter helplessness, believing God can save and change, so that the heart delights in His will. That is what it means to be "born again." This meant that Nicodemus had to let go of all his vain efforts and religious striving and simply *believe* or *trust* in this rabbi from Galilee, that He would save him.

Soteriology, study of salvation, is as vast and deep a topic as one can imagine. On the surface, it's a rather simple concept, the death of the righteous so that the unrighteous may be pardoned, yet its implications will be pondered throughout eternity. In addition, what actually took place on the cross as Christ died in our place can be looked at from so many different angles, it may simply overwhelm us. For our purposes, we will attempt to explain *why* salvation is necessary and then look at its effects and implications on our lives by highlighting the following theological terms: *reconciliation, justification, regeneration, sanctification,* and *redemption*. Using these terms is not my attempt to sound intelligent or "talk like I got sum learning." Rather, these are

---

[52] Psalm 40:5–8 NLT

terms that the Scripture uses, and it is my desire to make these terms more accessible and familiar to the average Christian. If we can appreciate the full weight of what is being communicated in Scripture by better understanding these terms, we can also better appreciate the salvation we have in Jesus Christ.

Reconciliation

Simply put, sin separates. We see this in even the closest of relationships. Let's say you have two people who have been best friends for years, and one is caught lying about the other with another group in order to gain acceptance. That obvious betrayal will void, at least temporarily, any trust that once existed between the two close friends. There would be feelings of betrayal, pain, and anger. The sin of the one friend has caused a rift that will only be healed when, and if, the offended party is willing to forgive.

What's true in human relationships is also true in the Divine relationship. Our sin against God, however, is so much more grievous than a petty lie told out of convenience. In fact, even what we would consider our more *acceptable* sins are more comparable to rape, murder, or molestation in the eyes of God. And those sins certainly have the power to separate. Our sin, both inherent and committed, has made separation from God the norm, and there is absolutely nothing we, as the offending party, can do to repair that relationship. R.E.O. White writes, "Sin affects God, so as to require from him judgement, withdrawal, correction, creating for God too a barrier to fellowship, a problem to be resolved before God and sinful humanity can be at one again."[53]

Surprisingly, God's response, throughout scripture, to our sin is one of forgiveness, compassion, and relentless devotion. It was God who came down to seek out Adam and Eve as they hid; it was

---

[53] Walter A. Elwell, ed., *Evangelical Dictionary of Theology* (Grand Rapids, Michigan: Baker Academic, 2001), 993.

God who spoke to a man named Abram when the world was given over to idolatry; it was God who came down to deliver His people from Egypt by the hand of Moses; and, it was God who, through the prophets, called out to, corrected, and wept over His people seeking to bring them back to Himself. Ultimately, it was God who clothed Himself in human flesh and dwelt among His people in order to seek and save those who were lost. Jesus expressed the heart of God as he wept over Jerusalem, "O Jerusalem, Jerusalem, the one who kills the prophets and stones those who are sent to her! How often I wanted to gather your children together, as a hen gathers her chicks under her wings, but you were not willing!"[54]

Paul succinctly sums up the problem and the solution in Colossians 1:21, "And you, who once were *alienated* and hostile in mind, doing evil deeds, he has now *reconciled* in his body of flesh by his death, in order to present you holy and blameless and above reproach before him." Our sin has alienated us from a holy God and requires judgement. That judgement was meted out on the cross as the sinless Son of God, took on the sin of the world, and experienced our separation, so that we could be made righteous, and thus, experience a relationship with God.

Justification

You cannot have reconciliation without justification. *Justification* is the acceptance of one as right in the eyes of God. 2 Corinthians 5:21 which says, "For He made Him who knew no sin to be sin for us, that we might become the righteousness of God in Him." The doctrine of justification is one that can be difficult for us to swallow because pride says, "I can fix this... I'm a pretty good person... I'm not that bad... God should accept me." On the other hand, the Bible says, "There is none who seeks

---

[54] Matthew 23:37

after God," and "All our righteousness are like filthy rags."[55] The Bible has declared us guilty despite our best efforts to fix or excuse ourselves.

As a result, we cannot stand in the presence of a holy and just God. Let me illustrate. I have two Labrador retrievers, Jalen and Healer, that my wife and I adore. One night, a few teenage boys camped behind our house, and the next day Jalen, Healer, and I did our normal walk. When we returned to the house, I was suddenly overwhelmed by the most god-awful smell. I checked my shoes, the trash can, and finally—the dogs. They had eaten some of the *leftovers* from the campout, and by, leftovers, I do not mean food. Evidently, they had found where the boys used the bathroom the night before. Immediately, I threw the dogs outside, washed their mouths out with the water hose, and threw out a whole bag of doggy breath biscuits. They did not come back into the house for three days! What they had done and how it had tainted them was simply too offensive for them to remain in the house.

Now, in much the same way, our sin is far too offensive for us to be able to enjoy fellowship with God. Also, just like I was the one who had to clean the dogs and get them to the point where they could eventually come back into house, God is the One who makes us right, so that we may enter into and enjoy His presence. Finally, if I had left the dogs to themselves, they would have probably gone back to the leftovers, and maybe even rolled around in some dead animal to boot, and in a dog's mind, those things are just great! In the same way our attempts to fix ourselves, to make ourselves acceptable in the eyes of God, are all the more offensive. We are completely unable to justify ourselves; it is God who has to take the initiative.

Since we cannot obtain the righteousness or justification God

---

[55] Romans 3:11 & Isiah 64:6

requires for fellowship, He *imputes*[56] to us righteousness or treats us as if we are righteous. However, the question we must struggle with is this, "On what grounds can God declare an unjust and offensive sinner just?" Remember, God is *just,* and just as we would never stand for the unconditional release of a child rapist, God, too, demands justice. Jesus Christ came and lived a perfectly righteous life and died our death in order to fulfill the demands of God's justice. The Bible is replete with the idea of *substitutionary atonement.* For example, the spotless lamb being offered in the Temple for the sins of the worshiper. Our sins, therefore, are dealt with in the death of Christ, but the perfect life He lived is also given or imputed to us so in God's eyes, we are declared righteous!

The means of that justification is faith in the person and work of Jesus. The great Reformer Martin Luther beat his head against a wall trying to find justification before God, only to come to the conclusion that all his efforts were useless. "How can a sinner enter into fellowship with a holy and righteous God?" Luther found this to be an impossibility. He shares his frustration,

> For I hated that phrase "the righteousness of God" ... by which God is righteous, and punishes sinners... Although I lived an irreproachable life as a monk, I felt I was a sinner with an uneasy conscience before God; nor was I able to believe I had pleased him... I did not love—in fact, I hated—that righteous God who punishes sinners.[57]

He knew the demands of a holy God, "...you shall be perfect, just as your Father in heaven is perfect,"[58] and it drove him crazy

---

[56] Romans 4
[57] Alister E. McGrath, *Luther's Theology of the Cross* (Malden, MA: Blackwell Publishing, 1990), 96.
[58] Matthew 5:48

because he knew he would never live up to those demands. He felt it unfair for God to demand of us something we would never achieve. After much seeking and anguish the reformer read the prophet Habakkuk; "The just shall live by his faith."[59] The cry of the Reformation became "solo fide,"—"faith alone." One is not made just or righteous by their actions but by their faith in the One who is just. Being justified by faith means that one understands their failure to meet the requirements of God's Law, admits this, and looks to Christ who fulfilled those requirements in their place. The Apostle Paul lays it out clearly in Romans;

> For all have sinned and fall short of the glory of God, *being justified freely by His grace through the redemption that is in Christ Jesus,* whom God set forth *as a propitiation by His blood, through faith,* to demonstrate His righteousness.[60]

He also writes, "Therefore, having been justified *by faith*, we have *peace* with God through our Lord Jesus Christ, through who we have access *by faith* into this grace in which we stand."[61] God's righteousness, therefore, was not one we could earn or obtain but one that was modeled by Christ and then bestowed upon us in grace through faith in Him.

The individual who has put their faith in Christ understands their guilt and their impending doom. They also know they are utterly helpless in their attempt to be freed. However, another has, in essence, paid the price that they may be declared righteous before God and have peace with Him. Martin Luther called this the "great exchange." Jesus's righteousness is *imputed* to us and our sin is laid upon Him. This all serves the greater purpose of showing forth God's righteousness and bringing him glory.

---

[59] Habakkuk 2:4

[60] Romans 3:23–25; *italics mine*

[61] Romans 5:1–2a; *italics mine*

Being declared righteous removes my guilt and gives me the great privilege of engaging in fellowship with God. The frustration of trying to live up to an impossible standard can be laid aside. I can stand before God *not* because of my flawless performance but because of Jesus! *He* has made me righteous! I don't have to constantly chase a better version of myself or a more fulfilling stage in life. I have all I need in Jesus!

Regeneration

Sin is not just something we do wrong or something we should have done but failed to do. It is a part of our nature. Calvinistic theology speaks of "total depravity" which essentially teaches that every aspect of man - his mind, his will, his emotions - have been corrupted by sin. The prophet Jeremiah confirms this truth stating, "The heart is deceitful above all things, and desperately wicked. Who can know it?"[62] Not one person has been exempted from this problem and all sane people would admit their shortcomings. The simple cliché, "No one's perfect," is proof of that.

Regeneration is the transformation of the heart, the birth of a "new man," so the individual who once rebelled against God now has an underlying desire to please God. Paul writes, "Therefore, if anyone is in Christ, he is a new creation; old things have passed way; behold all things have become new."[63] This is one of the things that distinguishes Christianity from every other religion on the planet. The philosophy of this age, and many other religions teach that mankind is at his core good, and we must seek, through education, enlightenment, spiritual awareness, religious devotion, or self-discipline, to develop and encourage that goodness. In contrast, Christianity teaches that human nature is so marred by sin that it cannot be salvaged; it must be replaced.

---

[62] Jeremiah 17:9

[63] 2 Corinthians 5:17

35

The objection to this goes something like: "People have improved themselves through education, spirituality, or hard work, haven't they?" Outwardly speaking, that may be true. However, the heart's desire has never changed. We are selfish at the core and one's education, spirituality, or hard work are only means by which one pursues their functional god (or what they really worship), be that peace, fulfillment, prosperity, prestige, acceptance, possessions, power, pleasure, etc.

Having been made new does not mean that we are completely free from what we used to be. The "old man" is still present within our being, and we will deal with this until the day we meet Jesus face to face. Paul speaks constantly of the battle with the flesh.[64] However, we must not lose heart. The only way we lose this battle is to stop fighting. This is part of the ultimate struggle of coming to know God more intimately. It is our human frailty that clouds our vision of God and hinders our fellowship with Him. That is why the old nature must be dealt with on a daily basis, as we allow the Word of God to correct us, as we allow the Holy Spirit to reveal our weakness, as we consistently confess our sins, and as we submit ourselves to our Father in fervent prayer and worship.

Sanctification

Some have said there are three tenses to salvation: I have been saved, I am being saved, and I will be saved. I am not sure how theologically correct this may be, but I think it does portray the truth about salvation presented in Scripture. For the Christian, justification and regeneration can be spoken of in the past tense, "I have been justified before God… I now want to please God, and before I did not." Our next term may also be spoken of in past tense, but it carries with it an ongoing responsibility. *Sanctification* simply means being set apart. All who have been saved are set

---

[64] Romans 7:7–25; 2 Corinthians 10:3–9; Galatians 5:16–26

apart. We are set apart from what we used to be. We are set apart as His people, the Church. In addition, we are also set apart for His work in the world.

However, being set apart also means to be made holy. Now, because we have been justified, we have a "borrowed" righteousness, and, positionally, we are holy in the sight of God. But, practically, we are *not* holy. Martin Luther said it this way, "at one and the same time righteous and a sinner." The evidence of that is seen every time we miss the mark of God's righteousness, in every debased thought, and in every impure motive. This is why Paul writes in Thessalonians, "For this is the will of God, your *sanctification*."[65] He then warns them to avoid sexual immorality. In essence Paul was saying, "God wants you to grow in holiness and in righteousness and avoid sin," and if one has been regenerated, deep down they want that too. Just as a baby grows and matures, changing month by month and year by year, so too, does the sincere Christian.

If there isn't growth, maturity, or "fruit" in the life of a Christian then their faith may rightly be questioned. James wrote an entire epistle on Christian maturity, sanctification, and *real* faith, pointing out that real faith in Christ manifest itself in good deeds, controlling one's mouth, humility, wisdom, dependence on God, fervent prayer, and accountability. Paul says a growing Christian will exhibit *love*, which manifests itself in joy, peace, longsuffering, kindness, goodness, faithfulness, gentleness, and self-control.

As we examine our lives through prayer, in the Word, with the aid of the Holy Spirit, and in the context of authentic Christian fellowship, let us struggle with the question, "Are we growing in holiness?" Here is where the depth of our relationship with God is measured. Remember sin separates us from God, but there is still a part of us that doesn't mind that. We want forgiveness, but

---

[65] 1 Thessalonians 4:3; *italics mine*

we know as we draw nearer to God, it requires we deal radically with sin in our lives; there are just some sins we've excused or justified for too long. They've become part of who we are, and we're comfortable with them. So our relationship with God becomes superficial, stagnant, and eventually nonexistent.

In my late teens, I came home late from time to time after having a few (well, several) beers with my friends. When I would walk in, of course, my mom was waiting up for me. At that point I had a decision to make. Do I go straight back to my room and avoid her altogether, raising her suspicions, or do I sit down and talk with her so she will think everything is cool? Being the seventeen-year-old genesis I thought I was, I would sit on the couch on the opposite side of the living room and attempt to engage in conversation. I didn't want to get too close because I didn't want her to smell me but I didn't want to go straight to my room and risk her coming back there to question me. Of course she likely knew what was going on, praying I would come clean rather than continue my pretense.

I think we treat God in much the same way. We want to be just close enough to God to ease our conscience and feel good about ourselves but not too close because we know deep down there will be things brought to the surface that we must deal with.

John Owen's book, *The Mortification of Sin,* pulls no punches when speaking of sin; "Do you mortify [sin]; do you make it your daily work; be always at it whilst you live; cease not a day from this work; be killing sin, or it will be killing you."[66] There is a tension here; sin keeps us away from God, while at the same time, we can't rightly deal with sin unless we come close to God. Through Christ we have access to the Father, whereby He calls us to Himself that our sin may be obvious and there we repent of it! We do not defend or excuse it, *we repent and seek the power*

---

[66] John Owen, *The Mortification of Sin* (Ross-shire, Scotland: Christian Focus, 2010), 26.

to change. This is majestically portrayed in Isaiah's life when he is standing in the Temple, and suddenly the holy presence of God fills the room. Isaiah, who was a holy man, responded the only way he could, "Woe is me, for I am undone! Because I am a man of unclean lips…"[67] Isaiah's sin becomes all the more obvious in God's presence. *God* then cleanses Isaiah's lips and God does the same for us as we draw near to Him confessing our sin for "He is faithful and just to forgive us our sins and to cleanse us from all unrighteousness."[68]

With that said, look at the questions posed by Paul in Romans 6:1 & 15, "Shall we continue in sin that grace may abound… Shall we sin because we are not under the law but under grace? Certainly not!" We don't get the full impact of that last phrase in the English but Paul's answer to these questions is blunt, "This cannot be!" In other words: You cannot keep on purposely sinning and call yourself a Christian. He goes on to say the proof of your faith is seen in whomever yield yourself to. If you yield yourself to God, then you are a child of God, but if you yield yourself to sin, then sin is your master. Flee temptation, fight sin, and draw near to God!

Redemption

Probably the most intimate term regarding salvation is the term *redemption*. *Redemption* refers to a ransom being paid in order to pay off the debt of a family member. While justification says we are made right in God's eyes, redemption draws us to God's side and calls us family. Our sins incur an insurmountable debt that we can never repay but God in His mercy pays that debt for us. Here we see God as the Father who weeps over the slavery of His children and is willing to pay any price to free them. Speaking of

---

[67] Isaiah 6:5
[68] 1 John 1:9

God as Father Peter writes, "Knowing that you were not redeemed [purchased] with corruptible things, like silver or gold...but with the precious blood of Christ."[69] Ephesians chapter one tells us we have been *adopted* as sons! The All-powerful and Holy God calls us sons! We don't just have the opportunity to grovel at His feet but the privilege to sit in His lap!

This redemption is two-fold according to Ephesians chapter one. First, it is the forgiveness of sin[70] whereby we are pardoned and accepted much like the prodigal who returned to his father in humility hoping to be a servant only to find himself completely restored as a son. Second, while we enjoy fellowship with God here and now, it is partial at best, for we have yet to see Him face to face. In ancient times, people would often pay a redemption price, then later return to take possession of what was purchased earlier. I think this is what Paul had in mind when he wrote, "You were sealed with the Holy Spirit of promise, who is the guarantee of our inheritance *until* the redemption of the purchased possession, to the praise of His glory."[71] One day Christ will return to take possession of what He purchased on the cross two thousand years ago, and in that day we shall see Him as He is and be made like Him, glorified and perfected in reality not just in position. Then our salvation will be fully realized. Praise God!

---

[69] 1 Peter 1:18–19a

[70] Ephesians 1:7

[71] Ibid, v. 14; *italics mine*

4

God

And God said to Moses, "I AM THAT I AM." —Exodus 3:14

He's on up in age now, and what he used to be seems like a whole other life, but he thinks about it every now and then. How could he not? He has nearly all day to himself watching over sheep that aren't even his in the middle of nowhere. He was well-educated, and in the best schools no less. Philosophy, theology, astronomy, science, languages, and law, he mastered them all. He hobnobbed with society's elites and even garnered their admiration. Once, a long time ago, he was beyond respected; he was feared. He led armies to glorious victories, returning home to parades in his honor. He was even being groomed as royalty, as a prince of the greatest empire on earth: Egypt. Then one day he walked (well, ran) away from it all.

Moses wasn't an Egyptian and he knew that. While he rose in the ranks of Egyptian society, his people, the Hebrews, suffered in slavery. Who knows how long it gnawed at him, but one day something inside him had had enough, and he took it upon himself to act. He killed a man. He assumed that his people would see what he was trying to do. After all, he garnered the respect of the royal house. How hard must it be to gain the respect of a bunch of slaves? Instead, they wondered, "Who does this Egyptian think he is?" When it was discovered what Moses had done, he had no choice but to run and run he did, for thousands of miles until he ended up in Midian.

But that was a long time ago, and Moses had grown to love this simple life. He'd married, had couple of kids, and Egypt had become nothing more than faded memory. All of that was about to change. With his face wrapped and his head slightly tucked, he pushed his way through the sand storm. "Much longer and these sheep will have to fend for themselves," he murmured. Finally, the storm broke and Moses found himself at the base of *the* mountain.

His wife's family had told him that this was the mountain of God, but Moses was skeptical. Oh, he knew the gods of Egypt, but he always thought of them more in terms of bedtime stories, especially since he knew all the tricks the so-called priests used to convince the people. He had also heard the Hebrew slaves speak of *a* God, but what god would allow his people to languish in slavery? Thinking back on his brethren, he felt something once, the voice of the God? An overwhelming compassion? Who knows? BUT he acted on it, and here—here he was on the back side of nowhere leading sheep rather than men.

As Moses gathered the sheep and began to head home something caught his eye. Up on that mountain, the one all his wife's family was afraid to go near, he saw what looked like a fire. "There's something different about this fire," he thought, "Wonder what it could be?" So Moses turned aside to investigate. When he reached the place, he had to shield his eyes, but he could tell it was an acacia bush. It was burning with the most brilliant fire he had ever seen, yet the bush was not consumed.

Moses warily approached the bush and suddenly heard, "Moses, Moses!" Startled, Moses responded the only way he could. He stuttered, "It...it...It's me." As he draws near, the voice says, "Don't come any closer, take off your sandals, you are standing on holy ground…I am the God of your father - the God of Abraham, Isaac, & Jacob."[72]

"Could it be?" Moses wonders. Some of his people had told stories about this God, but those stories were said to be from over 400 years ago and who knows what the truth really was. Even most of the Hebrews felt like those stories were nothing more than fairy tales. As Moses struggled to believe what he was seeing and hearing, the voice spoke with both authority and compassion, "I have surely seen the oppression of My people who *are* in Egypt, and have heard their cry because of their taskmasters, for I know their sorrows. So I have come down to deliver them out of the hand of the Egyptians."[73] That feeling that Moses felt over 40 years ago came rushing back to him but this time it was as if it were a thousand times heavier. For some reason Moses' heart felt shattered.

"I will send you to Egypt to deliver My people," the voice uttered but Moses was done with Egypt. His life was here now. Besides, he was nearly 80 years old, and all the bravado and confidence he once had was long gone. In addition, he had tried once, and the people wanted nothing to do with him. Finally, as Moses considered the command, he asked, "Who shall I tell them sent me?" Probably thinking, "I can't very well tell them the 'bush' sent me." God responded, "I AM WHO I AM."[74]

More than an Idea

In our culture, God is nothing more than some vague idea, a solely benign being in the sky who is rather harmless. The creation could be God, a divine "watch maker" who sits aloft in the heavens waiting to see what happens, or maybe you are God,

---

[72] Exodus 3:5–6 NLT

[73] Ibid, vs. 7–8

[74] Ibid, v. 14

in a sense? For Moses, it may not have been much different. The stories of the Egyptian gods were, to be sure, fantastic, but he felt they were nothing more than stories. The Hebrew God seemed so distant, if He existed at all. And, the God of the mountain his in-laws spoke of was down-right scary. Whatever worked— Maybe the Hebrews' belief in their God gave them hope, surely the stories of Egyptian gods inspired people, and the God of the mountain, well, he kept those rough and wild shepherds in line.

What Moses faced in the burning bush was not an idea but a living Being of infinite power and knowledge. This was not a god shaped by the will, inclinations, or the fantasies of man. He was much more than inspiration or hope, or even someone to whom one was accountable. This was the great "I AM!" The One that spoke to Moses revealed Himself so that He may be known not just speculated or assumed.

The One True God

For us, this is a struggle because we can easily comfort ourselves with a god of our imagination and this God that Moses met is just way too big, way too powerful, and much too sovereign for us. He is not accountable to us nor will He be manipulated. Our only response to a God like this can be that of submission to whom He *is* not what we wish Him to be.

Over the next few pages I want us to set aside our preconceptions about who we feel God to be. I want us to struggle with who He *is*. Remember: this is ultimately a struggle to surrender, to acknowledge our utter incompetence and complete dependence. The win is not that we somehow overcome God or figure Him out. It is not even that we overcome life's obstacles and difficulties but that we are humbled by God's immense power, love, and holiness, so we come to know Him more fully.

As we briefly examine *Theology Proper*, please remember it

is not my purpose to give a full orbed theology of God but to highlight aspects of His being that challenge us, humble us, encourage us, and ultimately put us in awe of Him, so that we have no other choice but to fall to our face, humble our lives, and worship Him.

The Revelation of God

The book of Hebrews makes the following statement, which is very telling about the nature of God: "See that you do not refuse Him who speaks."[75] God is a speaking God and throughout Scripture, God seeks to make Himself known while man seems to avoid God in favor of other gods. In fact, the Bible is rather clear and blunt on this point; "No one is acceptable to God! Not one of them understands or even searches for God. They have all turned away and are worthless."[76] Despite man's hardness, God's heart is still to reveal Himself. Quoting A.J. Heschel, A.J. Conyers writes, "God is not a being detached from man to be sought after, but a power that seek, pursues, and calls upon man [and] Revelation is the moment in which God succeeded in reaching man."[77]

In Scripture, we see this play out over and over. When Adam and Eve sinned, they hid themselves while God came down and called out to them. When the world was plunged into idolatry, God revealed Himself to a man named Abram. When God's people sinned again and again, He sent prophets pleading with the people to repent and return to Him. In each case, we see God going out of His way to make Himself and His will known. There are two major ways in which God does this: general or natural revelation and special revelation.

---

75 Hebrews 12:25
76 Romans 3:1012 CEV
77 Conyers, *A Basic Christian Theology*, 17.

General Revelation

Psalm 19:1 states the heavens declare the glory of God and Romans 1:20 says that His power and nature are clearly perceived in the things that are created. Whether you are talking about perfect position and condition of the planet enabling it to support life, the complexity of the cell, the nature of the atom, or the beauty of nature itself, it takes more faith to believe all of it was an accident than to see it for what it is: the deliberate, ordered (although fallen) creation of God.

In addition to creation, there is also the existence of morality. Now, many may disagree with this, stating that morality is some short of social construct, but in reality all of us appeal to some universal law that defines right and wrong. Granted, there are major disagreements in the culture war on what right and wrong is, whether you are discussing abortion, gay marriage, the redistribution of wealth, or the subsidizing of certain social programs. However, even in these disagreements people on each side are appealing to some higher standard; Fairness, compassion, equal opportunity, personal rights, etc. Deep down all sane people would agree that the rape and/or murder of an innocent child is horrific. Today, most people, thanks in large part to Christianity, agree that the enslavement of another person is unjust and wicked. There are things that, even in our fallen condition, we know are wrong.

On the flip side most people would say it is good and/or right to help others in need. C.S. Lewis delves into this by using the example of someone in danger.[78] As that individual cries out we probably have two desires: one, to help and the other to keep out of danger. Lewis then states that along with those we also have something that tells us we should follow the impulse to help and suppress the impulse to save ourselves. This is what he called

---

[78] Lewis, *Mere Christianity*, 22-23.

"Moral Law" and another way in which God has revealed Himself to us in *general revelation*. What we do with that revelation truly matters. Do we accept it as God speaking to us or ignore it setting God aside in order to pursue our own ideas, passions, and desires?

Special Revelation

While general revelation says there is a God, special revelation tells us who that God is. For Christians this special revelation is the Bible. There are at least two main passages in the Bible that serve as the foundation for the Christian understanding of Scripture: 2 Timothy 3:16–17 & 2 Peter 1:20–21. 2 Timothy states,

> All Scripture is given by inspiration of God, and is profitable for doctrine, for reproof, for correction, for instruction in righteousness, that the man of God may be complete, thoroughly equipped for every good work.

This passage reveals several things about Scripture to us but it also raises a few questions.

First, it states that Scripture is *given* by the inspiration of God. Again, this is God initiating the conversation, God reaching out and giving Himself to humanity. In addition, Scripture is not of human origin, but "God-breathed." Thus, it has the authority to instruct mankind as to whom God is and what He expects. It also has the authority to reprove and correct us, as difficult as that may be to accept. With that said, these questions are then raised, *What exactly is Scripture? How do we know which books or letters in the Bible, if any, are "God-breathed?"* These are questions we will address in the chapter on the Bible. Long story short, throughout history Scripture has more than proven itself to have a supernatural origin.

While 2 Timothy gives us the ultimate origin of Scripture, Peter gives us the method by which God chose to give us the Scripture. He writes,

> Knowing this first, that no prophecy of Scripture is of any private interpretation, for prophecy never came by the will of man, but holy men of God spoke as they were moved by the Holy Spirit.[79]

Essentially, God, the Holy Spirit, moved or "carried" these men along, using their personalities and experiences, to reveal Himself to humanity. Again, God is taking the initiative to reveal Himself even though He is under no obligation to do so.

This passage tells us no one person or group of people has a corner on the market when it comes to knowing and understanding God. The Bible was written by both royalty and peasants, farmers and shepherds, priests and reluctant loners, a once respected Pharisee and a despised tax collector, some ignorant fishermen and some religious zealots, a rejected missionary and one gentile doctor. Many of these men struggled with God's revelation. In fact, if you look at the messages of men like Moses, Jeremiah, Habakkuk, or Paul, you would think they could have found a more appealing message. For example, Jeremiah was branded a trader for preaching that the idolatry and injustice of his people would lead to their captivity at the hands of the Babylonians. Paul was beaten on countless occasions, stoned nearly to death, jailed numerous times, thrown out of cities, and shipwrecked, yet he still continued to proclaim the same message. This is just a testament of the truth that these men proclaimed and wrote about. Through

---

[79] 2 Peter 1:20–21

the Scripture penned by these men, God reaches out in order to establish a relationship with His creation.

The Otherness of God

As we examine the passages of Scripture that show a merciful and loving God "coming down" in order to restore man and a God who seeks, through nature and Scripture, to reveal Himself, it is possible for us to become too comfortable with Him. In fact, we may even begin to believe that God is just a better, more perfect version of humanity. Nothing could be further from the truth. There is a real fear that many in our churches today know nothing of trembling before God. It is popular to casually think of God as friend or Father, and God is very much those things. However, *we cannot simply jump from enemy of God to friend unless we are first overwhelmed and shattered by His holiness.*

We prefer a God we can manipulate, one who is benign and reassuring, one who is very much like us but more righteous and understanding. And by understanding, I mean, a God who really doesn't hold us accountable for our wrongs and just reassures us. Like the Israelites leaving Egypt, we have created a god we are comfortable with because the real God, the LORD, is just too scary. The Psalmist wrote, "You thought I [God] was altogether like you; But I will rebuke you."[80] God is not one of us and an understanding of His holiness should bring us to our knees in utter desperation.

When the Bible says God is "holy," we shouldn't simply overlook that or grow accustom to the term. The word holy means *separate* but when used in relation to God it also includes God's transcendence and His purity. God is completely *other than* anything. When we speak of the *otherness* of God then, we speak of His separateness, His purity, His moral & personal perfection,

---

[80] Psalm 50:21

49

His complete independence, His unwavering justice… His glory! There is nothing like Him, nothing to compare to Him. No one can fully understand and explain Him.

What, then, is the response of the Christian to the otherness of God? There is a passage from Job that helps us here. It both declares God's holiness and glory and shows the only response man can give. Job has suffered much loss, sickness, and has been accused of wickedness by his friends. He begins to question himself and God, and God's response is epic!

> Who is this who darkens counsel by words without knowledge? Now prepare yourself like a man; I will question you, and you shall answer Me. "Where were you when I laid the foundations of the earth? Tell Me, if you have understanding. Who determined its measurements? Surely you know! Or who stretched the line upon it? To what were its foundations fastened? Or who laid its cornerstone, When the morning stars sang together, And all the sons of God shouted for joy… Have you commanded the morning since your days began, And caused the dawn to know its place…Have you entered the springs of the sea? Or have you walked in search of the depths? Have the gates of death been revealed to you? Or have you seen the doors of the shadow of death? Have you comprehended the breadth of the earth? Tell Me, if you know all this.[81]

Notice Jobs response: "Behold, I am vile; What shall I answer You? I lay my hand over my mouth." He is utterly overwhelmed and helpless. Isaiah saw the glory of the LORD fill the Temple

---

[81] Job 38:2ff

in his day. The angels declared, "Holy, holy, holy is the LORD of hosts; The whole earth is full of His glory!"[82] In the words of R.C. Sproul, "In that single moment, all of his self-esteem was shattered. In a brief second he was exposed, made naked beneath the gaze of the absolute standard of holiness."[83] Isaiah could only respond, "Woe is me for I am undone!" Both Job and Isaiah saw themselves in contrast to the holiness of God and knew they were worthless and in the cross hairs of God's just wrath and there was nothing they could say or do.

The otherness of God demands our repentance and worship, and by worship, we mean our adoration and the full submission of our lives. As overwhelming and almost scary as God's holiness is, our acknowledgement of our helplessness and our repentance invokes His pity and mercy. It is God's desire to forgive and restore us to Himself, to make us holy, to call us His children. However, *we must first worship Him in His holiness before we can walk with Him in fellowship.*

God's Sovereignty

As Jesus stood in the hall of Pilate, a representative of the mighty Roman Empire, he remained silent despite the Roman governor's questions. To Pilate, Jesus was nothing more than a peasant, a nuisance and he wanted to get to the bottom of the situation as quickly as possible. Growing frustrated Pilate attempted to intimidate Jesus, "Do you not know that I have the power to crucify you?" After repeated silence and apparently unintimidated, Jesus finally speaks up, "You could have no power at all against Me unless it had been given you from above."[84] Jesus' point was clear: You are not in control here. My Father is and

---

[82] Isaiah 6:3

[83] Sproul, *The Holiness of God*, Kindle ed.

[84] John 19:11

51

everything that happens from here on out will happen according to His plan.

When theologians speak of the sovereignty of God, they simply mean that *God is in control.* There is nothing that happens in history that he has not planned and ordained. Granted there is some element of mystery here because we are left to question whether or not we have free will. It is not my mission to unravel this mystery, but let's just say that the Bible emphasizes both God's absolute control over history and human responsibility. We have freedom, but God's freedom and His purposes are greater and will not be thwarted by our choices. In fact, God uses our choices, both good and bad, for His greater purposes. Not to mention that He is fully aware of what those choices will be. Thus, God's sovereignty shouldn't concern us or be a source of debate but should be something that actually comforts the Christian because *none of life is insignificant or wasted when lived under the purposeful and all-powerful hands of a loving Heavenly Father.*

History bears out God's sovereignty. Look at the great Empires of the ancient world: Nebuchadnezzar of Babylon, Cyrus of Persia, & Alexander the Great of Greece. All of these men thought they were expanding their own empires, spreading their influence, and establishing a name for themselves. However, these great empires of history were actually being wielded by God for His purposes. Babylon was being used by God to bring judgement upon His people, Israel. Look at the warning of Jeremiah,

> Behold, *I will* bring a nation against you from afar... They shall destroy your fortified cities, in which you trust, with the sword... [because] you have forsaken Me... Now *I have given* all these lands into the hand of Nebuchadnezzar the king of Babylon, *My servant.*[85]

---

[85] Jeremiah 5:15, 17, 18; 26:6 ESV; *italics mine*

God called the powerful Nebuchadnezzar His servant. Then when he would become proud and create a statue of himself to be worshiped, God would cause him to go insane. Babylon eventually falls to Cyrus of Persia whom Isaiah calls "anointed" and through Isaiah the LORD said he was the one "whose right hand I take hold of to subdue nations before him...for the sake of Jacob my servant, of Israel my chosen."[86] God would use Cyrus to send His people back home where they would rebuild their city and the Temple. Alexander would eventually conquer Persia, and in doing so, would spread the Greek language from Europe to northern Africa, to the Middle East, and all the way to India. The books of the New Testament would be written in Greek, a language, by that time, accessible to almost everyone in the ancient world, one that was precise, and perfect for conveying abstract ideas. Even mighty Rome was used by God because the same roads built to quickly move Rome's army from place to place would be used to carry the Gospel of Jesus Christ.

Revelation 13:8 describes Jesus by stating He was "the Lamb slain from the foundation of the world." His crucifixion was not a tragedy nor an unforeseen accident. It was planned and foretold and God centers all of history around it. Do you actually think that God was shocked by Adam and Eve's disobedience? No! In fact, God speaks to the ultimate solution right there in the Garden: "And I will put enmity between you and the woman, and between your seed and her Seed; He shall bruise your head, and you shall bruise His heel."[87] The seed of the woman (i.e. Jesus) will strike a deadly blow to the head of the serpent while the serpent will only manage to land a temporary injury to His heal. In Acts, Peter and John declare that Jesus was delivered up to be crucified

---

[86] Isaiah 45:1 & 4 NIV
[87] Genesis 3:15

by the "determined purpose and foreknowledge of God."[88] The central point of all history is the cross and it was not plan B.

When we are tried with difficulty or blessed with success, we must remember who brought about these circumstances. God owns the situation! Like Jacob who was promised by God that he would return home, we too must remember God still has a purpose for our lives no matter what we suffer, what difficulty we face, or even what prosperity we enjoy. God is not shocked by what comes into our lives, rather it has first come through His hands. When the unexpected happens or tragedy strikes, unlike us, God is not running around panicked, wondering how He is going to deal with this. Romans 8:28 reminds us of that. "We know that all things work together for good to those who love God, to those who are the called according to His purpose." God uses *all* things for our good and His glory. Real faith stands firm knowing *He is in control and none of life is insignificant or wasted when lived under the all-powerful and purposeful hand of our loving Heavenly Father.*

---

[88] Acts 2:23

5

The Bible

*And so we have a prophetic word confirmed, which you do well
to heed as light that shines in a dark place.* —2 Peter 1:19a

In the twelfth year of his reign, Josiah, who at that time was
only twenty years old, took on a huge task: rid his nation of
idolatry. He tore down the altars and images of false gods
throughout the land and ground them into dust. He searched
out the secret places of worship up in the hills and destroyed
them. Josiah even dug up the bones of pagan priests and had
them burned. He was a man on a mission. However, it wasn't
until the eighteenth year of his reign that he began to truly
reestablish the true worship of Yahweh.

Following the order of the king, workers begin to purge
and repair the Temple. As they start the demolition, light slips
through a crack into a hidden hallow inside the wall and fell
upon a scroll. It was a copy of the Law of Moses—probably the
book of Deuteronomy. As the priest reads the Law, Josiah senses
imminent danger for his nation. He hears, "If you do not obey the
voice of the LORD your God...these curses will come upon you."
Among these curses were, "Your sons and daughters shall be given
to another people...a nation whom you have not known shall

eat the fruit of your land."[89] About eighty years earlier, Judah's sister nation, Israel, was conquered by the Assyrians and led into captivity. In Josiah's day, the mighty nation of Babylon stands on the doorstep of Judah, and Josiah could very easily envision all of the things promised in Deuteronomy taking place.

In addition, the years prior to Josiah's reign were certainly nothing to brag about when it came to Judah's relationship with God. Josiah's predecessor, Manasseh, had plunged the nation into one of its darkest periods as idolatry became the norm. He rebuilt pagan places of worship in the mountains where the worship likely included sexual orgies and child sacrifice. He also encouraged the use of soothsaying, witchcraft, and mediums. The second book of Kings chapter twenty-one verse nine says, "Manasseh seduced them to do more evil than the nations whom the LORD had destroyed before the children of Israel." As the priest reads aloud all the things that would bring about Judah's destruction, Josiah had to be thinking, "My nation has indulged in every one of these things! WE. ARE. DOOMED."

Josiah's response upon hearing God's Word was swift, "The king stood by a pillar and made a covenant before the LORD, to follow the LORD... with all his heart and soul, to perform the words of this covenant."[90] Standing by the pillar of Solomon's Temple, Josiah sought to reestablish the covenant his people had made with the LORD so many years ago. After the covenant renewal, he finished purifying and renovating the Temple. He also continues to search out pagan priests and pagan worship centers in his attempts to heed the book of the Law. "There was no king like him, who turned to the LORD with all his heart, with all his soul, and with all his might."[91]

Imagine for a moment the crushing weight of imminent

---

[89] Deuteronomy 28:32–33
[90] 2 Kings 23:3
[91] 2 Kings 23:25

judgement. You're caught in the act of infidelity, you've broken the covenant you made with your spouse, and you know your marriage is over. This isn't the first time, and your spouse has promised time and again they were leaving and that time has finally come. Your children are devastated, your spouse will live forever with the pain, and your family will be torn apart. This is where Josiah was as the Word of God was read. He knew his nation had "played the harlot" for too long and God had no choice but to be faithful to His Word.

The crushing reality of the Word of God is that it doesn't hold back, it shows us exactly who and what we are, and who God is. Our only response to its truth is that of submission and a plea for mercy. Josiah struggled to accept what was read because he knew judgement was coming. He struggled as he attempted to align himself and his nation with the Word. Think about it. These people had been led around by their perverted passions for years. They enjoyed the priestess prostitutes and other indulgences. They did whatever they felt like doing and now this young, prudish king was going to take all of that away. He must have wrestled in this as the people fought him, and for all his strenuous labor, he was promised the impending judgement would not come during his life time.

Just as Josiah struggled to align his nation with the Words written in the Law, we too struggle to accept the Bible's truth, turn from our perverted and comfortable ways, and pursue transformation through God's Word. However, God has promised mercy to the humble and repentant. Everyone falls short in their obedience to God's Law, but that Law was never intended to save us or earn God's blessing. Its purpose was to show us ourselves, show us God, and bring us to repentance. It was given in love as God sought to reveal Himself and His character to us. Its truth often pains us, just as it did Josiah, but it also preserves and strengthens those who seek to live by its commands. We all have turned to other "gods" and deserve the judgement coming to us, but the Bible brings "Good News" in that God, in the person of Jesus Christ, has taken upon Himself the judgement we rightly deserve and granted those who trust Him mercy, grace, and righteousness.

Questioning the Bible

For Christians, the Bible is foundational to our faith. But, what makes the Bible so special? Why is it any different from other holy books or writings? How can we trust that the Bible is what it claims to be? How can we trust that the Bible we have is God-inspired Scripture?

These are serious questions I've wrestled with personally, and I can attest to the desire to nail these concerns down before taking Christianity seriously. After all, this is what the Christian faith is based upon. While you can never know anything with one hundred percent certainty, after years of study, I've come to the conclusion that the evidence is heavily in favor of the Bible's Divine origin.

Now, it is not my purpose to provide a comprehensive apologetic on the inspiration and reliability of the Bible, but in the next few paragraphs, I want to offer some evidences to encourage us against the assaults of modern day critics and spur us to continue our struggle in maintaining the Bible's Divine inspiration, reliability, and relevance. Assuming that Jesus is who He said He was, the Son of God, and that He gave the Apostles the unique authority to establish the early church through their teaching, let's look briefly at how their writings were preserved.

The New Testament

Historically, the transmission of the Bible cannot be matched. There are nearly 6,000 copies of New Testament fragments and several complete copies ranging from 300s to the 1500s A.D. in existence, which is more than any other ancient text. And, many of those other texts are anywhere from 600 to 900 years separated from their original authors. Because of the tremendous amount of New Testament material, it is possible to use this material to create an accurate manuscript that matches what was originally written by the Apostles and other Biblical authors with up to 99.4 percent accuracy.[92] In other words, you can use all the manuscripts and copies to weed out minor mistakes and figure out which texts are the variants compared to what the authors originally wrote.

However, if you listen to critics like Bart Erhman, you will know that many of these manuscripts do have a lot of discrepancies.[93] What you may not realize, though, is the majority of the differences are very miniscule and include things like minor differences in punctuations, spelling differences, and phrase reversals. Almost none of these differences changes the text significantly.

The Gospels were written by men who knew Jesus or one of the close associates of the Apostles. They record the life of Christ and highlight His sacrificial death and ultimate resurrection. The book of Acts was a continuation of the book of Luke and records the history of the early church up until about twenty or twenty-five years after Jesus' death. The remainder of the New Testament is made up of letters written from one of the Apostles to the churches in which they ministered all over the Mediterranean world. These letters address doctrinal issues, practical problems with the local congregations, and provide instruction and encouragement for the believers.

The early churches kept these letters along with one or more of the Gospels and read them regularly. When the letters would

---

[92] Daniel B. Wallace, *New Testament Textual Criticism*, Cross Examined podcast. https://crossexamined.org/podcast_new-testament-textual-criticism-with-dr-daniel-b-wallace/

[93] Bart Erhman, *Bible Contradictions*, Monotheism Disproved, Youtube.

wear out they would have them recopied word for word in order to preserve them. In the second and third centuries, several new letters began popping up under very familiar names like Thomas, Judas, Peter, Barnabas, etc. Eventually, many of the church leaders got together to weed out these *pseudepigrapha* or false autographs and identify the genuine Gospels and letters. They asked four questions: 1. Was the letter written by an Apostle or close associate? 2. Was it widely used and accepted and thus have a trusted pedigree? 3. Did it contradict known Scripture and doctrine? 4. Was it inspired? In 300s A.D., the council of Church leaders agreed upon the twenty-seven books of the New Testament we have today, most of which were included in previous lists from other church leaders as far back as the first century.

The Old Testament

While most of the New Testament was written within about thirty or forty years, the Old Testament was brought together under the sovereignty of God over a period of about 1000 years. Moses authored the first five books called the *Torah* around 1400 B.C. Over the next 1000 years, many other prophets, kings, song writers, and historical scribes would add to it. Many scholars believe that most of the Old Testament was pulled together during the Babylonian captivity circa 550 B.C. A few other books, like Esther, Ezra, Nehemiah, and Malachi would be added as the Jews returned to their homeland, but by the 400s B.C., the Old Testament is considered closed until the preaching of John the Baptist.

When it comes to archeological evidence, the Old Testament has proven itself reliable time and again. When the Dead Sea Scrolls were discovered, they contained every Old Testament book but one,[94] and they were over a thousand years older than the

---

[94] The one book not included was the book of Esther.

accepted *Masoretic Text*. Yet, there were hardly any differences worth noting between the two Hebrew texts. For years, scholars maintained that there was no such Babylonian king named Belshazzar, as portrayed in the book of Daniel, because Nabonidus was known to be the last king of Babylon. However, archeological discoveries proved that Belshazzar did rule as a co-regent with his father Nabonidus.[95] In addition, the Assyrian king, Sargon, mentioned by Isaiah was also believed by scholars to be made-up, as was his conquering of Ashdod, but once again, archeology bore witness to the truth of the Bible when in the 1800s his palace was discovered in Iraq. In addition, in 1963, a stele was found which recorded his victory over Ashdod.

Why the Bible?

For the Christian, the Bible is the final authority on matters of faith and life in that it tells us what we should believe and how we should live. Remember, Paul tells us in 2 Timothy 3:16-17 that all scripture is "God Breathed" which means the Spirit of God did not simply use these men like a pen to write His Word but "carried" them along using their vocabulary and personalities. Because of its inspiration, Paul states that it is "profitable" to us in several different ways. First, the Bible provides correct teaching on what Christians should believe; second and third, it calls out our sin and tells us how to correct it; finally, it instructs the Christian on how to live righteously. Boiled down to one statement: *Scripture has a supernatural origin, and it is where our knowledge of God comes from and is that sure foundation upon which we can build our lives.*

The ultimate end in our study of scripture is twofold. First, Paul says the man of God may be "perfect" or mature. Second, it equips us for His work. We are born again as babes in Christ,

---

[95] Walter Kaiser Jr. & Duane Garrett, ed. *NIV, Archaeological Study Bible: An Illustrated Biblical History and Culture* (City, Company, Year), pg. 1393.

but we are not to remain babies. It is God's desire that we grow in our faith and mature into active and fruitful Christians. That is done as we accept the truth of scripture and allow the Holy Spirit to change us by it. James writes, "Receive with meekness the implanted Word, which is able to save your souls."[96] In the same vein Paul says, "Be transformed by the renewing of your mind that you may prove what is that good and acceptable and perfect will of God."[97]

As I write this, my son, Kross is about fifteen months old. He has been walking for about 4 months and is now beginning to expand his vocabulary. Every time he says "Mama" or tells us what a horse says or even growls like the Incredible Hulk, my wife, his grandparents, and I think it is the greatest thing. However, by the time he is fifteen, I hope he is beyond growling like the Hulk. By that time, he should have some modicum of athletic ability, show respect to his elders, be able to do Algebra, embrace responsibilities around the house, and have somewhat of an adult conversation. In the same way, Christians use the Bible to "grow up" into what God has called them to be. Too often our churches are filled with immature, unstable, uncommitted, inconsistent "Christians" who have no idea what maturity is, nor any desire to grow in their faith. As a result, they remain like children: selfish, easily offended, quarrelsome, and fruitless. The hard work of maturity begins with getting into the Word, soaking it in, and allowing the Holy Spirit to use it to challenge and change us. The writer of Hebrews suggests that growth along these lines is a struggle when he writes,

> For though by this time you ought to be teachers, you have need again for someone to teach you the elementary principles of the oracles of God,

---

[96] James 1:21
[97] Romans 12:2

and you have come to need milk and not solid food. For everyone who partakes only of milk is not accustomed to the word of righteousness, *for he is an infant.* But solid food is for the mature, who *because of practice* have their senses trained to discern good and evil. Therefore, leaving the elementary teaching about the Christ, *let us press on to maturity...*[98]

God's Word is our nourishment. Peter tells us that we should desire the pure milk of the Word, that we may grow by it. Unfortunately, we live in a time similar to that which Amos spoke of; "Not a famine for bread or a thirst for water, but rather for hearing the words of the LORD."[99] Notice Amos doesn't say there's a famine of the Word but for the "hearing" of the Word, for the digesting of the Word. It's one thing to look at a plate of food, admire it, comment on how good it looks and smells, or even analyze its nutritional components, but it's quite another thing to actually eat that food. Just like our physical diet, it is often the best food we like the least. It takes discipline to eat right just like it takes a disciplined and consistent devotional life to partake of the Word of God on a daily basis.

Not only do we digest the Word, allowing it to supernaturally change us, but we also seek to obey the Word or put it into practice. Just as a healthy lifestyle includes both a proper diet and exercise so does a healthy Christian life. Our proper diet is the Word of God read, prayed over, and meditated upon. Our exercise is that we do what the Word says which usually goes against what is natural and easy for us. Just like exercise takes discipline and effort, the practice of God's Word can be just such a challenge. That is why Paul, using an exercise metaphor states, "I discipline

---

[98] Hebrews 5:12–6:1 NASB; *italics mine*
[99] Amos 8:11

my body and bring it into subjection…"[100] However, just as with physical exercise the more we do it, the easier it becomes. Yet, both Christians and athletes keep pushing themselves, recognizing and overcoming weakness (through His grace) and continually strengthening that which is good.

In addition to maturity, Paul also states the Word equips us "for every good work."[101] If Jesus modeled for us anything, it was humble service to others. As a Christian, we are not to live in isolation but are to become part of the greater body called the Church. Salvation in and of itself is not the end game; we are to make a difference in the culture in which we live as we seek to fulfill His purposes. Jesus said in John 15 that it is the Father's desire that we bear "much fruit" and that that fruit should remain. The fruit he speaks of here could possibly include, Godly character, good works, and more Christians.

The purpose of the Church is to make Christ known through the proclamation of the Gospel, our growing Godly character, and our service to others. We must seek to equip ourselves for this task. Anyone who starts a new job and desires to be successful will first seek to understand what that job requires, then try to prepare themselves for that job through study and practice. When we become Christians, it involves more than sitting on a pew on Sunday morning. There is a great work to be done, and we all must seek, through God's Word, to equip ourselves for it.

Just as Josiah used the book of the Law to fight back the growing darkness in his nation, we too must lay ourselves bear before the Word of God, allowing it to expose our weaknesses while at the same time strengthening us to slay the beast within. The Bible speaks of the "old man" and the "new man" of which the Christian is composed. Being born again, we now have new desires to please God and live righteously. However, the old man,

---

[100] 1 Corinthians 9:27
[101] 2 Timothy 3:16–17

or the flesh, is still present within us causing conflict in the new man. Paul calls us to "crucify" the old man with its desires.[102] In part, we do that by doing that which the Word commands. Overcoming evil with good so to speak.

In addition, the Bible is described as a sword that cuts through our fleshly façade and our vain pretentions right into our inner most thoughts and motives. It leaves the "old man" exposed and defenseless. Exposed by God's Word, we can no longer offer excuses or justification for sin and shortcomings. We can only offer repentance and a plea for God's mercy. In that state God gives grace to humble, grace to grow and change, and equipping grace for the work of His Kingdom.[103]

When Paul left the Colossian church, he was surely concerned about their continued growth as new believers. It was his hope that through God's Word, with the aid of the Holy Spirit, believers would be transformed from mere babes in Christ to mature believers equipped for God's service. It must have been encouraging when he got a good report for he writes,

> I am with you in spirit, rejoicing to see *your good discipline and the stability of your faith in Christ*...as you have received Christ Jesus the Lord, so walk in Him, having been *firmly rooted and now being built up in Him and established in your faith, just as you were instructed.*[104]

These people had obviously feasted well on the Word of God and were growing as a result.

---

[102] Galatians 5:24

[103] 1 Corinthians 15:10; *Romans* 12:3–8

[104] Colossians 2:5–7a NASB; *italics mine*

Four M's

Your relationship with the Word will determine your level of spiritual maturity so make that relationship sure. Warren Wiersbe wrote,

> For those who want to "be strong in the Lord and in the power of His might" (Eph. 6:10), religious fast food is unacceptable. We must "take time to be holy," and that means taking time to receive and digest the milk, bread, meat, and honey of the Word.[105]

Here are 4 M's to help you get into the Word and the Word to get into you.

One: *Mark* you Bible as you read it daily. Make you a place and take time to get alone with the Word of God and *don't just mark your Bible but let it mark you.* As God's Word, it has power to both challenge and change you. Humble yourself before it and let it do just that.

Two: *Memorize* the scriptures. Pick some keys verses (not just ones that make you feel good either) and attempt to memorize them to the best of your ability. This puts God's Word at your disposal as a weapon against the forces of darkness. It also gets it in your Spirit and your mind where it can initiate change.

Three: *Meditate* on the Scriptures. This is another way of getting God's Word into your spirit. In addition, you find that as you do this the Holy Spirit has an uncanny ability to use the Scriptures to speak to the current circumstances of your life. You can meditate by asking questions of text, reading study guides or commentaries, listening to your pastor's Sunday sermon again, and by praying over the text.

---

[105] Warren Wiersbe, *Being a Child of God* (Nashville, TN: Thomas Nelson Inc., 1996), 62–63.

Four: *Move* on the Word. This is where the struggle to let the Bible directly influence our lives takes place. Both the study and the practice of God's Word is essential if we are to grow in our faith and equip ourselves for service. Let us accept the challenge of James, "But be doers of the word, and not hearers only, deceiving yourselves."[106]

---

[106] James 1:22

6

Prayer

You have hidden yourself in a cloud so our prayers
cannot reach you. —Lamentations 3:44 NLT

He had heard enough! Pashhur was the overseer of the Temple grounds, and this so called "prophet" had disrupted things for the last time. He walked out into the courtyard, and in one quick motion, he drew back his fist and laid into Jeremiah, catching him off guard and knocking him to the ground. Immediately, he called for the temple guards to put him in stocks. "Let's see if a night in stocks won't change your tune!" barks Pashhur.

Jeremiah spent the night locked up in the stocks. The next day, with his wrists and ankles bleeding, Jeremiah was brought back to be questioned by Pashhur again. Before Pashhur could say anything, Jeremiah declared, "God has a new name for you: not Pashur but Danger-Everywhere."[107] Jeremiah went on to explain that because Judah's spiritual leaders, like Pashhur, refused to tell the truth, they were the real terror in Judah. In addition, Jeremiah repeated the message that got him thrown in the stocks to start with; "I [the LORD] will hand the people of Judah over to the king of Babylon. He will take them captive to Babylon or run them

---

[107] Jeremiah 20:3 MSG

through with the sword."[108] Then, as to add insult to injury, he continued, "As for you, Pashhur, you and all your household will go as captives to Babylon. There you will die and be buried…"[109]

As soon as the words left Jeremiah's mouth, he wished he could pull them back before they reached Pashhur's ears, but it's likely he'd spend another night in the stocks. There Jeremiah complained or prayed, "You pushed me into this, God, and I let you do it. You were too much for me. And now I'm a public joke. They all poke fun at me."[110] Jeremiah went so far as to promise he won't speak again in the name of God because all God gave him is doom and gloom. However, he quickly realized if he did that, it would become "fire in his bones" and he could not help but speak. Throughout his prayer Jeremiah cursed the day he was born, prayed for vengeance upon those who have mistreated him, and dreaded what laid ahead. However, he also sang to the Lord, gave God thanks for His felt presence, and acknowledged that deep down, he knows God is working everything out.

Jeremiah's life was difficult to say the least. He was given the unenviable task of warning Judah of its impending doom at the hands of the Babylonians. As a result, he endured much persecution. He was publicly ridiculed on numerous occasions. He was imprisoned at least twice and on one of those occasions he was lowered into a pit where he was left to die a slow death as he sank into the mud. In his on hometown he received death threats. Throughout his ministry, Jeremiah was beaten, not allowed to marry, and branded a trader by the false prophets whom he openly rebuked.

Through it all, however, Jeremiah maintained an authentic and consistent prayer life. Even when God seemed to ignore him Jeremiah continued to petition and even question God. He would

---

[108] Jeremiah 20:4 NLT

[109] Ibid, v. 6

[110] Jeremiah 20:7 MSG

accuse God of deceiving him, ignoring him, and even having it out for him but then, in the next breath would proclaim, "Sing to the LORD! Praise the LORD!"[111] He would question whether God knew what he was doing then say, "Ah, Lord God! Behold, You have made the heavens and the earth by Your great power...There is nothing too hard for You...You are great in counsel and mighty in work."[112] Jeremiah would even accuse God of wrapping Himself in a cloud, so as not to concern Himself with humanity, then he would write, "Your eyes are open to the ways of all mankind."[113] He would speak the truth with upmost boldness then weep and pray privately for God's people who wanted nothing to do with God.

We may never face the hardships that Jeremiah endured, but all of us struggle to understand and accept God's will. Sometimes it's all we can do to make it through the day. Meanwhile, seeking the will of God and aligning ourselves to it through prayer is the farthest thing from our minds. Jeremiah stood alone against kings, prophets, and his own people in his attempt to fulfill God's purposes for his life, but he was not alone. He confidently declares, "But the LORD is with me as a mighty, awesome One." He also knew that God knew his heart,[114] so he could pray humbly and honestly. For Jeremiah, prayer would not be an attempt to change the mind of God but a struggle that always ended with Jeremiah on the losing end. Even so, God welcomed Jeremiah's complaints, questions, and frustrations and often allowed Jeremiah to wallow in them. However, He did not leave Jeremiah there. As Jeremiah persisted in his prayers, God would always meet him there, further revealing Himself and changing the flawed and wounded prophet in the process.

Over the next few pages, we will attempt to explore what

---

[111] Jeremiah 20:13

[112] Jeremiah 32:17–19

[113] Jeremiah 32:19 NIV

[114] Jeremiah 17:9–10

prayer is, why we pray, what prayer can accomplish, and how we pray. My hope is that you will see how vital prayer is and be encouraged to engage in prayer on a consistent basis no matter the obstacles you face or the feelings you have on any given day. Prayer is not an obligation, but a privilege, whereby we can meet with our heavenly Father in real time and in real life.

The Privilege of Prayer

The *Westminster Shorter Catechism* begins, "*Question*: What is the chief end of man? *Answer*: Man's chief end is to glorify God and enjoy Him forever."[115] We were created so we might enjoy fellowship with God, but sin separated us from Him and devastated that awesome opportunity and privilege. However, God immediately sought to reestablish that relationship through the work of redemption, which is marvelously played out in the pages of Scripture. It begins with God coming down into the garden to search for Adam and Eve that He may, by blood, cover their sin. It culminates at the cross where Jesus, the God-man, gave His own blood to cleanse us of sin that we may have access into the presence of God. Prayer, then, is the means by which we get to enjoy the great privilege of God's fellowship and presence.

Unfortunately, in the Christian life, it is easy for prayer to be overlooked or ignored all together. Some may even feel that, practically, prayer doesn't accomplish very much. Sure, no one would openly admit this but if we were all honest with ourselves, we would have to say that prayer does not hold a prominent place in our lives. In fact, deep down, we see prayer as more of a burden than a pleasure unless, of course, we are visited by tragedy. Otherwise, we don't have time for it, or we put it off promising, "I'll get to it."

---

[115] The Orthodox Presbyterian Church, *The Westminster Shorter Catechism*, https://opc.org/sc.html. Accessed August 2018.

This sense of uselessness, the sense of prayer being unproductive, and our feelings of frustration stem from our misunderstanding of prayer. Prayer is not a tool by which we manipulate God in order to gain a favorable outcome in life nor is it a religious duty by which we earn points with God. There are two extremes to avoid in prayer: First, God sits disinterested in the heavens and our prayers are an effort to pry open His reluctant hand. Second, God answers all prayers in our favor so long as we have enough faith. The first extreme is anti-Biblical because in the Bible we see a God who is involved and responds when His people cry out. The latter reduces God to a cosmic bell-hop who is subject to our whims and desires so long as we have the right formula or an extraordinary amount of fervency. Speaking on the latter view of prayer, A.W. Tozer wrote, "Prayer among evangelical Christians is always in danger of becoming a glorified gold rush."[116] If we see prayer as simply a means to OUR desired end then, yes, we will likely find it burdensome and frustrating. *Prayer in its purest sense is about engaging in a real relationship with a real God.*

Principles of Prayer

People pray for all kinds of reasons. Maybe they are experiencing sickness or family issues. Maybe some pray in order to brag about how often they pray. Others expound upon their personal theology as they pray publicly. It could be that God doesn't seem to be reading the script they wrote for Him, so they pray to remind Him how life is supposed to go. Jesus clearly lays out the proper motivation for praying in Matthew 6:5-7. Look at *The Message* translation.

---

[116] Ronald Eggert, ed. *Tozer on Christian Leadership* (Camp Hill, PA: Christian Publications, Inc., 2001), April 15.

And when you come before God, don't turn that into a theatrical production either. All these people making a regular show out of their prayers, hoping for stardom! Do you think God sits in a box seat? Here's what I want you to do: Find a quiet, secluded place so you won't be tempted to role-play before God. Just be there as simply and honestly as you can manage. The focus will shift from you to God...The world is full of so-called prayer warriors who are prayer-ignorant. They're full of formulas and programs and advice, peddling techniques for getting what you want from God. Don't fall for that nonsense. This is your Father you are dealing with, and he knows better than you what you need.

There are a few key principles concerning prayer's purpose to take note of here. *First, prayer is not done as a show or to be seen or heard.* This was the purpose of prayer for the Pharisees in Jesus' day. He called them "play actors" because their prayers were nothing more than a performance soliciting the applause of other people. Unlike Jeremiah, these men were not honest before God, laying bear their raw emotions while questioning themselves and God. No, they only spoke with eloquent rhetoric, mostly praising themselves while throwing in the obligatory word of praise to God. Aside from the occasional admiration of the people, their prayer accomplished nothing.

Second, prayer is personal and authentic. Jesus tells His followers to find a quiet, secluded place and to be there as simply and honestly as they can manage. Here is where we see Jeremiah challenging God and questioning himself in one breath, while giving Him praise and finding peace in the next. This is the secret place of the Most High where we allow the Spirit of God to probe our inner most being exposing our prejudices and weaknesses.

Here, we openly confess our shortcomings, frustrations, sins, and questions to God while at the same time, seeking the power of His Spirit to change.

Third, prayer is not a formula or series of steps we invoke to get things from God. For many, this seems to be the primary reason we pray. We want God to do something for us, to give us something, or to change something for us. There is a place for that in prayer, but it is not prayer's primary purpose. Our day is not different from Jesus' day when He states, "They are full of formulas and programs and advice, peddling techniques for getting what you want from God."[117] Turn on Christian television today and you will see sermons and books full of "techniques" by which you can supposedly manipulate God in prayer with your faith and fervency. It's amazing how the great privilege of prayer has been cheapened and made into nothing more than a "glorified gold rush."

Finally, prayer is about relationship. Jesus says, "This is your Father you are dealing with..."[118] Never forget the high price paid that we may engage in a real relationship with God, our Father. Using the term "Father," Jesus highlights the fact that God is not an inaccessible, aloof deity but a personal Being deeply interested in our well-being and One who loves us beyond all imagining. In fact, He is endlessly working on our behalf. However, we don't always see it that way, thus Jesus adds, "He knows better than you what you need." Our heavenly Father knows what is best for us and much of prayer involves us discovering what that is and willingly submitting to it.

---

[117] Matthew 6:7 MSG
[118] Ibid, *v. 8*

Prayer Changes You

As with any good relationship, prayer should change you for the better. *If the purpose of prayer is fellowship, then the result of prayer is Christlikeness.* It has well been said the quality of our private prayer life will be seen in public. In other words, proper prayer will make us proper people, people who look like Jesus. As you pray rightly, you should see yourself as you really are and desire to be changed. As we enter the presence of a Holy God in prayer, we should be overwhelmed with a sense of our unholiness. It was Isaiah who cried, "Woe is me, for I am unclean," as he was confronted with the Holy presence of God. However, being "in Christ" we are seen as righteous/holy. The great reformer, Martin Luther said it this way, "Simul Justus et Peccator," or "at the same time a righteous person and a sinner."[119] The point being while we are rightly justified before God in Christ, we also still have sin in our lives.

Dealing with this sin begins with confession, which is often a missing element in our prayers. God's desire is to change us as we pray and that transformation begins with an honest examination of ourselves in the presence of a Holy God. It's easy for us to see the flaws and sins of others, but real prayer will focus more on our own sins than the sins of those around us. Jesus instructs us to first remove the plank from our own eye before removing a speck from someone else's eye. However, the enemy, Satan, will do all in his power to keep us focused on the sins and flaws of our fellow man. In his book, *The Screwtape Letters*, C.S. Lewis tells a fictional story of an older demon instructing a younger demon on this matter;

---

[119] Alister McGrath, *Christianity's Dangerous Idea* (New York, NT: HaperOne, 2008), 43.

> You must bring him [the new Christian] to a condition in which he can practice self-examination for an hour without discovering any of those facts about himself which are perfectly clear to anyone who has ever lived in the same house with him or worked in the same office.[120]

He goes on to mention the new Christian's relationship with his mother by stating that his attention must be kept on her "sins," which can be anything that inconveniences or irritates him.

While our attention is hardly ever turned away from others' sins, there are those rare moments when we recognize we have things we have to work on. We often meet that truth with anything but pure and honest confession. Rather, we offer excuses or justifications for our shortcomings, and we rarely call them what they really are: sin. We rationalize our motives and give ourselves way too much grace: presuming, "God understands." Maybe we compare ourselves to Hitler and remind God that we aren't that bad. All of this is nonsense. God calls us to confess our sins and repent, or turn away from them. To justify ourselves before a Holy God in prayer is the height of hubris. We're no better than the Pharisee who thanked God that he was not like the tax collector. This Pharisee, Jesus openly condemned. In authentic prayer, our only response can be that of devastation and a plea for mercy.

As we pray, we must remember we are dealing with a God that is working out all things for His glory and our good. The often quoted verse from Romans 8:28 says, "We know that all things work together for good to those who love God, to those who are the called according to His purpose." Usually, this is put on a coffee mug or hung sentimentally on a wall. Many understand it to mean, "God is going to work everything out." So, God will

---

[120] C.S. Lewis, *The Screwtape Letters* (New York, NY: HarperCollins Publishers, 2001), 12.

heal me, He will make my life easier after this difficulty, He will give me what I desire, He will make me rich, etc. In reality, we need only read the next verse to understand what "good" means to God. "For whom He foreknew, He also predestined to be *conformed to the image of His Son.*"[121] God's "good" for you is that you are conformed to the image of Christ. As we pray we must not see our suffering or difficulty as an obstacle to our determined end. It may well be that God is using those things to bring about HIS determined end which is that you become more like Jesus every day.

How We Pray

Jesus often withdrew from the crowds to pray. In Luke 11:1, Jesus returned from prayer, when his disciples requested: "Lord, teach us to pray." Certainly, this request pleased Jesus and without hesitation He began, "When you pray, say…"[122] What follows is a pattern that we can all follow. It includes praise, purpose, provision, pardon, and protection.

Let's begin with *praise.* Jesus' first words are, "Our Father…" Our attention and praise is not directed toward an impersonal deity that must be coerced into favors on our behalf. This is our "Father" who knows and desires what is best for us. As Christians, we do not grovel at God's feet like slaves. Rather, through Christ, we have been adopted and made the children of God. We have the right to cry "Abba, Father!" However, lest we become too familiar with God, Jesus adds, "…in heaven, Hallowed be Your name." The essence of what we see in many of the Psalms is that we enter the presence of God with praise on our lips and honor in hearts. Acknowledging that God is in heaven is included to "help us see our place – to humble us – and give us some objectivity about

---

[121] Romans 8:29; *italics mine*
[122] Luke 11:1–4

ourselves."[123] In addition, declaring His holiness reminds us of His otherness and our filth apart from Him.

Next, we pray with *purpose*. This is very clear and to the point as Jesus states, "Your kingdom come. Your will be done on earth as it is in heaven."[124] Hank Hanegraaff said it well; "Prayer is a means of bringing us into conformity with God's will, not a magic mantra that ensures God's conformity to ours."[125] Prayer is where Christian theology can be wrestled out, for it is in the place of prayer where we submit our will to the Lord's and seek transformation. Sometimes this is a painful and difficult struggle. It is in the moments of prayer when the "old man" is crucified and we surrender our will to God's. Christ modeled this in dramatic fashion when He prayed in the garden the night before His crucifixion. Through the sweat, agony, and blood, three times he asked His Father to take the cup of suffering from Him before He surrendered with the words, "Nevertheless, not as I will, but as You will."[126] Oh that we would pray with such purpose and passion!

From there, Jesus moves on to *provision*. Here, we acknowledge our ultimate dependence upon God and make our requests known to him. The Bible is clear. Our Father desires from us to ask of Him. Jesus says, "Ask, and it will be given to you; seek, and you will find; knock, and it will be opened to you. For everyone who asks receives, and he who seeks finds, and to him who knocks it will be opened."[127] He goes on to paint a picture of God, a good Father who wants to hear the requests of His children. However, like a good Father, He doesn't always give us what we want at the moment, but what is best for us. In our asking, our Father will

---

[123] R.T. Kendall. *The Lord's Prayer* (Ada, MI: Chosen Books, 2010), 61.

[124] Matthew 6:10

[125] Hank Hanegraaff. *The Prayer of Jesus: Secrets to Real Intimacy with God* (Nashville, TN: Thomas Nelson Inc., 2001), 46.

[126] Matthew 26:39

[127] Matthew 7:7

always answer, "Yes," "No," or "Later." We must trust He knows what is better than we do, what we need, and when we need it. In addition, we must understand that God is more concerned about our holiness than our happiness, thus *He gives what sanctifies us not always what satisfies us.*

Pardon is the essence of the Christian faith. Christians are a *forgiven* people, so it stands to reason that we should be a *forgiving* people. However, that is not always the case. Jesus tells a story of a man released from a debt of several hundred thousand dollars only to demand the imprisonment of a man who owed him the equivalent of twenty bucks. In the end, the first man who was forgiven such an enormous debt is thrown into prison himself. His unwillingness to forgive the debt of his fellow man only served to prove he never fully appreciated how much he had been forgiven. It is no different for the true Christian. The Christian who realizes the horrific nature of his sin against a holy God cannot help but be merciful because the sins against him are peanuts compared to his sins against God. Real prayer puts us in a position to see this ever so clearly and thus develop mercy towards those who sin against us.

Finally, we are instructed to pray for *protection*. As the Bible states on numerous occasions, we have an enemy that seeks our destruction. He is described as a devouring lion and beguiling serpent In addition, he is more powerful and smarter than we are. So, as we pray, we stay close to the One who is mightier and all-knowing, seeking His direction. After all, "He who is in you is greater than he who is in the world."[128] In addition to Satan, we also battle the world and our flesh.

"Lead us not into temptation," is a prayer that we be aware of Satan's devices and guard our eyes and our hearts. Through prayer, we struggle to deny the flesh and halt the influence of this age. We pray in our weak moments, we pray when we burn with lust, we

---

[128] 1 John 4:4

79

pray when we feel we got it figured out, we pray when we're about to lose our temper, we pray when we find ourselves too focused on the things of this life, we pray when we face sickness, frustration, unfair treatment, persecution, failure, success, unexpected riches, etc. All of these can be points of temptation. There may be times when we may feel we have gone too far down the road of temptation that we don't feel worthy to pray, but that is when we must pray. For our enemy, the great Accuser, would love nothing more than to keep us silent in those dreadful times.

Worship

As we conclude this chapter, there is an often overlooked aspect of prayer which should saturate our lives and that is worship. Matthew's version of the Lord's Prayer is bookended by worship. Like Luke, Matthew begins with "Our Father... Hallowed be Your name." However, he ends with, "For Yours is the kingdom and the power and the glory forever. Amen."[129] This is a declaration of God's glory, an acknowledgment of God's otherness and His complete ownership of all that exists. Worship cannot be limited to our times of prayer. As we discovered in the chapter on God, *worship is the adoration of God AND the full submission or our lives to Him.*

Worship is something that certainly begins in prayer but must be lived out in our daily lives. Romans 11:36–12:1 summarizes true worship in the life of the believer. Paul writes,

> For of Him and through Him and to Him are all things, to whom be glory forever. Amen. I beseech you therefore, brethren, by the mercies of God, that you present your bodies a living

---

[129] Matthew 6:13

sacrifice, holy, acceptable to God, which is your
reasonable service.

Keep in mind that in the Hebrew mindset, "sacrifice" equals
worship. When Paul says, "to who be glory forever," the word "glory"
means splendor, brightness, most exalted state, majesty, absolute
perfection, and/or preeminence. Knowing this Paul begs his readers
to "present" their bodies, their lives to God as a "living sacrifice."
This is an act of worship and reveals what is preeminent in our lives.

The human tendency is to present ourselves to things that
are far from glorious, and, thus, replace God with what has been
created. For example, possessions can become an obsession as
we find ourselves sacrificing the best of our time, money, and
efforts in order to obtain them. Our bellies can become a god as
we sacrifice our health in order to appease our appetite. We can
place the weight of God on other people, laying expectations
upon them they will never live up to. Thus, it becomes their job
to make us happy, bring fulfillment, or complete us. We may even
sacrifice our families in order to pursue the gods of money, power,
influence, and position in our jobs.

All of these acts of worship begin in the human heart, which
according to John Calvin is an idol factory. We offer ourselves to
these things daily, pursuing them on the false assumption they
will fulfill a deep seated need, bring fulfillment, or simply make
us happy. This is why prayer is so vital. It is in prayer where we
acknowledge our dependence upon God alone, it is in prayer where
we gain a true perspective that the things of this world are fading,
and it is in prayer where we are surrounded by the tangible presence
of God so that He and His power becomes real to us. Worshiping
God in prayer "magnifies the Lord" as the Psalmist wrote. It
doesn't make God any bigger than He is, it simply enlarges our
vision of Him so that He becomes the most preeminent thing in
our lives without rival. The battle for the heart will be fought and
won as we worship God in spirit and truth when we pray.

7

The Holy Spirit

*And I will pray the Father, and He will give you
another Helper, that He may abide with you forever—
the Spirit of Truth...* —John 14:16–17a

The last several weeks have both devastated and blown the minds of Jesus's followers. Jesus was crucified and buried, and as far as they know, his disciples will be next. Yes, Jesus had said he would rise again, but the reality is he is dead. He was an unmatched prophet, teacher, miracle worker—maybe more, but He's gone, and it almost seems surreal. It is over. The hopes and dreams of Jesus's followers are dashed. Many had thought He would restore Israel and usher in the long awaited Messianic Kingdom. Some just knew He would bring an end to Roman oppression, but once again, Rome proved to be too mighty. As despair sets in, Jesus lay in a sealed tomb marked a failure.

However, on the Sunday morning after His death, some of the women arrived at the tomb, and to their astonishment, the stone had been rolled away and the tomb was empty. At first, they thought someone had stolen his body. Suddenly, they were startled as two men declared, "He is not here, but is risen!" They then remembered Jesus' words, "The Son of Man must...

be crucified, and the third day rise again."[130] The women rushed to tell Peter and the other disciples, who immediately dismissed them as being overly dramatic. Peter, however, wondered, "What if they're right?" John, half way expected this and was already making his way to the tomb. As their expectations and hopes began to build, their hurried paces turned into an all-sprint. They arrived to find the tomb empty just as the women had described.

Over the next forty days, they would see Jesus on numerous occasions and they slowly began to grasp that His Kingdom was not of this world. During that time Jesus encouraged these men and women and instructed them about their mission to "make disciples of all nations."[131] Jesus even forgave Peter for denying Him during his trail. Then came the moment when Jesus will be taken up into the heavens. Surely, they didn't want to see him go a second time, but he had promised that He would not leave them "orphans" but that He will come to them. He would send the "Helper," the Holy Spirit.[132]

Jesus knew their mission would be difficult. He saw the rejection, the beatings, the jail time, the persecution, and yes, the martyrdom. At that moment, they're inspired and excited. Jesus had defeated death, and it was obvious He was exactly who He claimed to be: the Son of God! They watched him ascend into the clouds and Jesus left them with one last commandment, "Do not leave Jerusalem, *but wait* for the gift my Father promised."[133] Jesus knew they needed real power to endure persecution and to be effective witnesses of His life and message. The excitement they felt as they watched Him ascend into the heavens would be utterly inadequate for the task that lay ahead.

So… they wait. Ten days, they wait. Finally, on the day of Pentecost, the wind began to blow, the Holy Spirit descended,

---

[130] Luke 24:7

[131] Matthew 28:18

[132] John 14-16

[133] Acts 1:4 NIV; *Italics mine*

and Jesus' disciples were filled with power. Peter, the same man who denied Jesus when confronted by a teenage girl, stood and began to speak with an unusual boldness and wisdom. That day three thousand people were added to the church as a result of the Spirit of God moving and empowering the disciples.

Throughout the book of Acts we witness ordinary, humble people begin the process of literally changing the world. They face down both Jewish religious leaders and Roman officials as their freedom and their lives are threatened. A young deacon, named Stephen becomes the first martyr, stoned to death by a mob of Jewish accusers. John's brother, James, is executed by Herod. Peter & John spend more than one night in prison and carry the scars on their backs as a reminder. A young Pharisee, Saul, converts to the Way and suffers greatly on behalf of the Gospel. It seems like the more the world tries to stamp out Jesus's followers, the faster the Gospel spreads. It isn't mere determination or the triumph of the human spirit that enables this. It is the power of the Holy Spirit! Moreover, these people themselves were continually changed by that same power.

The Comforter

When Jesus begins to prepare His disciples for His departure, he begins with the famous statement, "Let not your heart be troubled…I go to prepare a place for you."[134] Now, the disciples obviously did not, at this time, fully grasp all that Jesus was communicating, but Jesus does make one thing clear, "I will not leave you orphans; I will come to you."[135] Throughout the remainder of the discourse, He mentions the "Paraklete" numerous times. This Greek term has been translated as *Comforter, Helper, Advocate,* & sometimes *Counselor* and is even the same name the

---

[134] John 14:1–2
[135] Ibid, v. 8

Bible uses for Jesus a few times. It simply means *one who comes alongside*. When we think of *comforter* or *counselor* we usually think of someone who comes to sympathize with us during a difficult time. However, the old English word for *comfort* is more closely related to the Latin, which is a combination of two words, *cum & forte*, which means *with strength*. So, the Holy Spirit is not so much one who comes to comfort us during the battle, but one who comes *with strength* for the battle. And, battle, we will.

When I was sixteen years old, my kidneys unexpectantly failed. I remember the moment I realized how serious it was. I was frustrated, angry, and scared. I was told I would have to have surgery immediately to insert a dialysis tube into my belly. For the better part of the next year I would spend my nights and an hour or two during the day hooked up to a machine that pumped fluid into my belly and drew it out again. This performed the function of my kidneys and cleansed my body of toxins. For a sixteen-year-old high schooler, it was a prison sentence.

As the doctor explained the seriousness of my situation and what the plan was, my whole life came to a screeching halt. I had no idea what lay ahead or how difficult and frustrating it would be. At that moment, my stepfather said, "Let's take a walk." He took me down to the hospital chapel where he knelt down and began to pray with me. He was a Marine, so it stands to reason I had never seen him pray out loud before and had definitely never seen him cry, but pray and cry, he did. When he finished his prayer, he looked at me and said something to the extent of, "We will get through this. These are very able doctors, and they have helped a lot of people in your same situation. Not to mention, God is more than able to help us through this." I'm not sure how much better I felt after that, but during the next eight or nine months, he nor my mother hardly left my side. They were there when I was in pain, they helped clean my wounds, questioned the doctors, sat up with me when I couldn't sleep, made me eat when I had no appetite, and on and on. My stepfather's presence gave me strength and reminded me that I wasn't alone. This is what Jesus means when He calls the Holy Spirit *Comforter*. Just as Jesus was Emmanuel, God with us, the Holy Spirit is God with and in us still.

The Work of the Spirit

The Holy Spirit is probably the most misunderstood person of the Godhead. However, His work in the life of the believer is absolutely essential and needs to be understood. An early theologian, Ambrose, called the Holy Spirit the "author of a new man."[136] As the author of a new man, the work of the Holy Spirit first begins with the *conviction* of sin. Second, the Spirit is the agent of *regeneration*. Third, the Holy Spirit is active in the *sanctification* of the believer. Finally, the Spirit *empowers* believers for service.

Charles Spurgeon sees the conviction of sin as an indispensable mark of the Spirit's work and suggests that "the new life as it enters the heart causes intense inward pain."[137] Conviction is more than mere remorse, for the human nature is not capable of the kind of conviction brought about by the Spirit. The Holy Spirit shows us our wretchedness in the sight of a Holy God and brings devastation to our souls. This rending of our heart, this unraveling of our being by God's Spirit leads to true repentance of sin.

Regeneration, seems to be an overlooked doctrine today. This is what Jesus called being "born again"[138] and what Paul called the "new creation."[139] It is the transformation of the heart, so that the once depraved and rebellious man, now wants to please God. The

---

[136] Ambrose, *On the Holy Spirit*, The Nicene and Post-Nicene Fathers, vol. 7 (Grand Rapids, MI: Wm. B. Erdmans Publising). Christian Ethereal Library, http://www.ccel.org/ccel/schaff/npnf210.i.html.

[137] Charles Spurgeon, *The Soul Winner* (SC: Bibilobazaar, 2008), 20.

[138] John 3:3

[139] 2 Corinthians 5:17

man who ran from God now desires God's presence in his life. The man who was unholy and only did what was right because of outside pressure, now struggles inwardly to *be* right. Now, there is some debate as to when this actually occurs but the Scripture is clear, the Holy Spirit does the work. It does not come about by any effort of our own. R.C. Sproul writes, "Regeneration by the Holy Spirit is a change. It is a radical change into a new kind of being."[140] As a result of His work our passions, motives, and desires are different.

Sanctification is another topic of the debate but most would agree that sanctification is growth in holiness and/or maturity. The man who is being sanctified is becoming more and more like Jesus in his spiritual walk, and the world has less and less of an influence in that saint's life. A.W. Tozer insisted, "The Holy Spirit never enters a man and then lets him live like the world."[141] The Holy Spirit is our constant companion as we mature in our faith. His presence often causes a struggle as we, through His power, seek to destroy the works of the flesh. It is through His strength we face every enemy with confidence, including the old man who will not go easily into the night. It is His Spirit that calls to us in order to draw us away from the way of the world. It is by the Spirit, through prayer, and as we draw upon the Word, that we assault the kingdom of darkness.

Finally, the Holy Spirit gives the Christian power, but not power in the way the world thinks of it. His power is not given that it may be used to dominate others but to serve others. The one indispensable evidence of the Holy Spirit's work and power in a man is his willingness to serve without recognition or worldly benefit. And he does so with a passion for the Gospel and the glory of God.

---

[140] R.C. Sproul, *The Mystery of the Holy Spirit* (Carol Stream, Illinois: Tyndale House Publishers Inc., 1990), 93.
[141] A.W. Tozer, *Tozer: Mystery of the Holy Spirit* (Alachua, Fl: Bridge Logos, 2007), 26.

In addition, this power was also a penetrating force that gave the Apostles boldness and wisdom in their proclamation of the Gospel. It is the Spirit's power in the believer's life that reaches heart where human words, works, and wisdom fail. Andrew Murray wrote, "Some preachers try to reach the hearts of their audience in the power of mere human earnestness, reasoning, & eloquence."[142] He goes on to say that preaching and the daily life will be a blessing to others when aided by the "full blessing of Pentecost," i.e. the power of the Spirit. Jesus was clear, "You shall receive *power* when the Holy Spirit has come upon you; and you shall be witnesses to Me...to the ends of the earth."[143] It is this power that carried the disciples through the early years of the Church, and it is this same power that is available to the Church today that we may effectively advance the Gospel in a hostile world.

The Holy Spirit and the Church

The Spirit's purpose coincides with the purpose of the Church: to make much of Jesus! In the Church, there is no room for loners or showoffs. The Church is *one* Body made up of many parts and each part has its particular function. Paul addresses this idea in great detail in 1 Corinthians 12–14. In in Ephesians 4, he writes, "Walk worthy of the calling with which you were called, with all lowliness and gentleness, with longsuffering, bearing with one another in love, endeavoring to keep the unity of the Spirit and the bond of peace." The Spirit brings unity to the Church, and when Paul speaks of lowliness, gentleness, & longsuffering, he is speaking of the characteristics of an individual dominated by the Spirit of God who is not seeking to make a name for themselves

---

[142] Andrew Murray, *Experiencing the Holy Spirit* (New Kensington, PA: Whitaker House), 1985, 27.
[143] Acts 1:8; *Italics mine*

but wants to see Jesus glorified and sees themselves as a servant to others. The power of the Spirit is not a me thing but a we thing. In Romans 12, Paul warns,

> [Do] not think of [yourself] more highly than [you] ought to think but think soberly... For as we have many members in one body, but all the members do not have the same function, so we being many, are one body in Christ, and individually members of one another.

The Holy Spirit binds Christian brothers and sisters together under the cause of Christ and gives them the power and the gifts to fulfill His commandment to make disciples. He does not make superstars or elevate some individuals over others. The spiritual gifts are to be used for the edification of the Church, not to draw attention to the more charismatic believers. The struggle and the passion of the Spirit-filled believer is the same as John the Baptizer: "He must increase, but I must decrease."[144]

In Romans 12, 1 Corinthians 12–14, and Ephesians 4, Paul makes it clear that the Spirit does give gifts and callings to individuals within the Church. The Holy Spirit gives gifts to advance the Gospel in the world, to edify the Church both corporately and individually, and ultimately glorify God. These gifts include, but are not necessarily limited to, words of wisdom, knowledge, faith, healing, miracles, prophecy, discernment, tongues, the interpretation of tongues, apostles, prophets, teachers, helps/service, encouragement, giving, leading, mercy, evangelism, and pastor teacher. Paul gives clear instruction that the gifts are to be used "decently and in order." The church is not supposed to be chaotic with everyone doing what they "feel" is right or even

---

[144] John 3:30

"spiritual." The gifts are to be used to make one more effective in their service to both sinner and saint.

Finally, Paul sought to combat spiritual elitism by showing the Corinthian church a "more excellent way." He spends nearly all of chapter thirteen in 1 Corinthians describing the true evidence of the Holy Spirit in a believer's life: *love in action*. Also, in a passage closely related to this, Galatians 5:22–26, Paul paints a vivid picture of what a truly "Spirit-filled" Christian looks like. In both passages, Paul expounds on the true nature of the God, which is selfless love. Yes, we should desire spiritual gifts, but we should "pursue"[145] love, meaning we should seek love eagerly, earnestly with an intense desire to acquire it.

Communion with the Spirit

At the risk of sounding mystical, I want us to get very practical concerning our relationship with the Holy Spirit. The Holy Spirit is God with us in a very real sense. In fact, it is His presence in our lives that often causes conflict and struggle within because our old man (i.e. the flesh) is at enmity with the Spirit of God that dwells in us. This is the struggle Paul speaks of in Romans 7 when he says, "For I do not understand my actions. For I do not do what I want, but I do the very things I hate." The Spirit of the Lord within man clashes with the desires of the flesh and does not allow for peace until the Christian yields.

The following chapter of Romans is a short Cliff Notes version of our lives in the Spirit. Paul begins by basically highlighting the limitations of the Law. The Spirit does what the Law could never do; He changes the heart of the believer, so now that believer is not only aware of sin but desires to please God and live righteously. Miraculously, we have the One who fulfilled the requirements of the Law living within us! Here's the struggle for the Christian:

---

[145] 1 Corinthians 14:1

Do we set our minds on the things of the flesh or the things of the Spirit? To set one's mind continually on the things of the flesh leads to internal turmoil and spiritual apathy or death. However, setting the mind on the things of the Spirit brings peace and life.

The Spirit also makes us "sons of God." This is important because we now have the right to approach God as our Father. As children of God, we have the privilege and liberty to approach God without fear of judgement no matter our struggles or shortcomings. The child of God runs to "Abba" in times of difficulty and even when we fail. That is what makes us spiritually-minded and evidences our Spirit-given desire to change and reflect the nature of our Heavenly Father.

Just as a child falls and scrapes a knee or breaks a bone, we may fail, but through the Spirit, we see it for what it is; sin. Sin is a defect in our nature that causes pain (inwardly, outwardly, and pain for God). Left untreated that scrape or break leads to infection or sickness. Avoiding sin would eventually lead to death. The child, rather than hide the skinned knee or ignore the broken bone, usually runs to their parent in pain and with tears wanting them to "make it better." The Spirit causes us to see our failures and flaws in just such a manner. Those who do not have the Spirit will never see sin like that. They will never think their sin is that serious nor will it cause them inward pain. So, they will excuse, justify, hide, ignore their sin, or compare themselves to others who seem worse. The Spirit makes us sensitive to sin and draws us to our Father to make it all better.

It is no secret life can be difficult and, at times, downright maddening. In addition, the world itself is full of suffering, sickness, and injustice. It is the Holy Spirit that reminds us this is not the way things are supposed to be. While giving us hope for a better future, the Spirit also uses our difficulties and suffering to shape us into the image of Christ. As we suffer and struggle, it is the Spirit that whispers, "Endure. You will make it to the other side of this more like Christ than when you started." It is the Spirit that reveals our weaknesses that we may take them to God and seek transformation. And, it is the Spirit who give us the power to be transformed.

God sovereignly orchestrates the circumstances of our lives in an effort to shape us. Thus, with our limited perspective, we may have no idea how to pray or what to pray for, so that is when we must lean into the Spirit and trust God with our lives. This is real faith; to ask God for something (healing, deliverance, or restoration) and trust Him even if He doesn't give it. That is what it means for "all things work together for [our] good." You need to know, however, that our "good" is not what is comfortable or pleasing to us but what make us like Jesus, and many times that is not pleasing to our flesh at all. However, as the flesh is mortified by suffering, the Spirit becomes more influential in our daily lives.

You will find no closer companion in this life than the Spirit of God. He loves us, and He loves Jesus's Church. The Spirit also empowers the Church to glorify Jesus through preaching of the Gospel and our service to saint and sinner. However, His power is infinitely greater than His ability to work miracles or give gifts. *The greatness of His power is seen in that He can take a wretched and sinful man and make Him a child of God through regeneration and subsequently transform that man so that he reflects the character and nature of Jesus Christ.*

8

Temptation

And do not lead us into temptation, but deliver us from the evil one. —Matthew 6:13a

Hunched over in the dark, he desperately attempts to grapple with what has happened. He has been unjustly accused of rape. As a slave, he should have been executed, but thankfully he's alive. Still, it doesn't seem fair because he will likely rot in this dungeon for something he didn't do. The crazy thing is he actually did what was honorable and right. Like a committed soldier, he served his master with dedication and loyalty. In fact, Potiphar's household had never run so smoothly nor had he ever been so prosperous, and it was all because of this young Hebrew named Joseph. He took his job seriously and took special care to avoid Potiphar's wife.

However, Potiphar's wife was not a woman to be denied something she wanted, and what she wanted was Joseph. He was young, handsome, and confident. Like a relentless fisherman, she kept dropping the bait, but Joseph wouldn't bite. He took great pains to avoid her whenever possible. He was never in the house alone with her and always tried to make sure one of the other servants was with him. This was not just a matter of trust between him and Potiphar, which was important, but for Joseph, he was driven by a deep reverence for his God. Giving in may have been pleasurable, and they may have gotten away with it but Joseph saw it for what it was: "great wickedness."[146]

One day, Potiphar's wife happened to find Joseph in the house alone and she pounced, demanding once more, "Sleep with me!" Joseph's heart raced as she ran her hands down his chest. He hesitated, but before the thought had a chance, he did the only thing he could think to do: He ran. In his haste, he unfortunately left some of his clothes behind. Scorned yet again, she had been rejected for the last time. Her desire for vengeance was fierce, and she screamed. As the echoes reverberated throughout the house, it drew the attention of the other servants, and when they arrived, she put on a show, weeping and trembling as she accused Joseph of trying to rape her. Potiphar was enraged. Whether it was because he believed his wife or knew she was lying, who knows? Either way Joseph was going to prison with his personal reputation shattered but his reverence to God intact.

Around nine hundred years later Israel's greatest king is home alone, relaxing on his rooftop. The Bible says it was at the time that the kings went out to battle. David should have been fighting with his men, but instead, he sent his general, Joab. The night was cool and clear. Seemingly every star was visible and God's glory was on display. David's attention, however, was elsewhere. As he surveyed the city which he essentially built, his eyes are drawn to a very beautiful woman bathing. Her figure was more than pleasing, and he doesn't turn away. Like a wolf eyeballing a potential kill, he takes it all in. Unable to control his urge, he sends for her, and a night of passion ensues ending with her back home in her own bed without being noticed. David enjoyed his moment, and no one would ever know.

However, his sin would not remain hidden. Bathsheba soon discovered she was pregnant. So David, in a desperate attempt to

---

[146] Genesis 39:9

cover his sin, sent a message to the battlefield for her husband, Uriah, to return home. After failing to get him to sleep with his wife, David sent him back to the battle front, patting him on the back with one hand, while giving him an official correspondence with the other. It was a command to Joab to have Uriah thrust into the hottest part of the battle and then have the other soldiers withdraw from him. The result was predictable. Uriah was killed while David made plans to marry Bathsheba.

Again, David thought he's in the clear, but nothing escapes the gaze of God. The prophet Nathan confronted the king with a story of a rich man whole stole a lamb from a poor man. David's rage over this injustice is ruthlessly unleashed as he declares that this "rich" man deserves death. Then in a most ironic twist, the prophet revealed, "YOU are the man!"

Upon hearing Nathan's declaration David cried out, "I have sinned!" Mercifully, he heard, "The Lord has put away your sin; you shall not die."[147] However, David would reap the consequences of giving in to temptation for the remainder of his life. The child he conceived with Bathsheba would die, and his home would be a disaster. His children would literally rape and murder one another, and one of his sons, Absalom, would successfully lead a rebellion to displace David as king.

David's sincere and heartbroken response is chronicled in the Psalms,

> Wash me thoroughly from *my iniquity*, and cleanse me from *my sin*. For *I acknowledge my transgressions*, and *my sin is always before me…* Hide your face from *my sins* and blot out all *my iniquities*. Create in me a clean heart, O God, and renew a steadfast spirit within me.[148]

---

147 2 Samuel 12:13
148 Psalm 51:2–3, 9–10; *italics mine*

Rather than shift blame or excuse his sin, David owned and acknowledged his sin for what it was, "iniquity." He sought God's forgiveness and moreover, he wanted the Lord to change him. David's response to his sin was exactly what God desired. This response to sin, sincere repentance, is the foundation of the Gospel proclaimed years later by Jesus Christ. Simply put, David humbly repented and sought God's mercy with "a broken spirit, a broken and contrite heart."[149]

An Obvious Struggle

Temptation seems to be the most obvious and difficult struggle in the life of a Christian. For every person who seeks to grow in their faith, this struggle is very real. Even Paul writes, "I want to do what is good, but I don't. I don't want to do what is wrong, but I do it anyway."[150] We get up every morning facing a number of decisions throughout the day: Decisions having to do with our work, our families, what to eat, what we watch, how we spend our free time, where we go, time spent with God, how we respond to conflict or compliments, how we deal with difficulty or the unexpected, etc. Underlying many of these decisions is a temptation: A temptation to do things *my* way or *God's* way, to do what is good and right or look for ways to excuse what is evil and easy, to give in to lust or flee and maintain purity, to be ruled by our emotions or be led by the Spirit, to become proud or humble ourselves.

Both Joseph and David faced decisions that effected the rest of their lives. By resisting temptation Joseph, in the long run, secured his position as the Prime Minister of Egypt and used it to preserve his family. By giving into temptation, David's home would be marked by chaos and conflict, his child from Bathsheba would

---

149 Psalm 51:17
150 Romans 7:19 NLT

die, and he would even lose his kingdom for a time. However, his repentance showed his sincere regret and desire to change. In fact, his humility, when confronted with his sin, was one of the things that made him a man after God's own heart.

The World and the Flesh

This is probably one of the more important chapters because it deals very practically with our sanctification and our relationship with God. *Our response to temptation often determines the trajectory of our spiritual growth and the level of intimacy with our heavenly Father.* However, if we are to overcome temptation we need to understand the enemies we face. Martin Luther revealed these enemies as the world, the flesh and the devil.

The term "world" in the New Testament may carry a few different meanings including the cosmos, the earth itself, the people of the world, etc. However, when the New Testament speaks of the world as our enemy, it's talking about a system that is opposed to God. Mark Bubeck calls the world system "a composite expression of the depravity of man and the intrigues of Satan's rule."[151] It is simply a combination of man's fleshly desires and Satan's influence. As such, man is constantly surrounded by that which feeds his depraved fleshly desires. The world demands we conform to its standards[152] and insists that pleasure, power, and prestige are sure ways to happiness and fulfillment. The world is wrong.

While the world's promises are alluring, it is the flesh that is all too eager to indulge in what the world offers. Biblically speaking, the flesh, sometimes called the "old man," is that compulsive inner force, which expresses itself in rebellion against God and His

---

[151] Mark I. Bubeck, *The Adversary* (Chicago, Il: Moody Publishers, 2013), 53.
[152] Romans 12:1–2

righteousness. It is the flesh that finds gratification in what God forbids. James places the blame for sin at the feet of our flesh when he writes, "Temptation comes from our own desires, which entices us and drags us away."[153] For the Christian, the flesh is that part of us that resists the Spirit of God that dwells within us.[154] These two will be forever in conflict until the day we see Jesus face-to-face.

Battling the Darkness

So, how do we battle these two ever-present foes? First, our response to the world is to be a light. Let's face it. This world will always be opposed to God. It simply awaits that day in which Jesus will return to expose its deficiency and tread the wine press of God's wrath on the system that has made so many false promises. Until that time, we are commanded to preach the Gospel and love our fellow man in very practical ways, praying for their salvation.

As we do this, we must also keep in mind that we are not to be "conformed" to the world. The world is like a strong river flowing in the wrong direction, away from God. It can be very easy to get caught up in that flow, allowing the world to influence your way of thinking and justify or excuse your sinful actions. We must combat this by what the Bible calls the renewing of our minds. Digest the Bible, meditate on it, accept and apply its truths, pray that your will is aligned to it, and, ultimately, let it be the thing that forges your convictions and shapes your character.

Finally, we are to endure the world. Jesus promises, "In the world you will have tribulation. But take heart; I have overcome the world."[155] The reality is that following Christ in a world that is hostile to Him will bring a great deal of discomfort, conflict,

---

[153] James 1:14 NLT
[154] Galatians 5:17
[155] John 16:33

and difficulty, but that is just a reminder that this world is not our true home.

The flesh, on the other hand, cannot be reformed, improved, or bargained with, it must be crucified. If we are to conquer the flesh, we are to first be honest with ourselves and with God. Francis Frangipane writes, "When we discover rebellion toward God within us, we must not defend or excuse ourselves…we must humble our hearts and repent, exercising our faith in God to change us."[156] This is more than mere confession but confession with intense sorrow for sin and a determined desire for change.

Next, we "reckon" ourselves dead to sin.[157] This simply means we deny ourselves the things and opportunities that bring gratification to the flesh. We guard our hearts, making a serious effort to filter what enters our hearts and minds. Practically, this means we are careful about what we watch on television, what conversations we engage in, how we pursue our finances, our use of the internet, the people we are close to, how we spend our free time, etc. This is what Paul means when he writes, "…casting down arguments and every high thing that exalts itself against the knowledge of God, bringing every thought into captivity to the obedience of Christ."[158]

Lastly, we "yield" ourselves to God.[159] This means that moment by moment, we look for opportunities to serve God. A bored man is a dangerous man. Find a good church to attend and serve in, serve the lost in your community, get involved in missions, seek to do your job with excellence, love and serve your fellowman, and if you are married, strive to be a godly husband and father, wife and mother. In this way, we are being proactive and not giving any space temptation to take root. Please note: the

---

[156] Francis Frangipane, *The Three Battle Grounds* (U.S.A. Advancing Church Publications, 1989), 17.

[157] Romans 6:11

[158] 2 Corinthians 10:5 KJV

[159] Romans 6:16 KJV

flesh is selfish and will seek to protect and defend its free time, its *little* indulgences and its *deserved* pleasures. This is a struggle of faith: to obey and yield yourself to God and deny the strong pull of the flesh.

The Devil

Satan, also called the devil, the father of lies, Lucifer, the accuser, adversary, or the evil one, is the ultimate source of temptation. From the very beginning, he has sought to distort God's Word and deceive God's people. In the Garden of Eden, he called into question God's command, then outright denied what God said was true, and finally, substituted a lie for the truth. He is subtle as he attacks our minds with lies designed to misrepresent God and deceive us into thinking there is a shortcut to pleasure, peace, prestige, fulfillment, or prosperity.

In John 10:10, Jesus brings Satan's tactics to the light stating, "The thief does not come except to steal, and to kill, and to destroy." This idea of a devil with a horns, pointed tail, and a pitch fork is far from the reality. In fact, Paul suggests that Satan and his temptations are quite attractive when he states, "Satan disguises himself as an angel of light."[160] This is why Jesus's statement is important. Satan's tactic is to make us think he's on our side, that he is for us and wants what makes us happy. Jesus, in essence, says, "As attractive as it may seem, don't be deceived, following the 'shortcut' leads to destruction."

First, Satan's goal is to kill us spiritually by getting us to believe his lies. For example:

- What's wrong with sex outside marriage if you love one another? [or] It's just for fun, don't be so moralistic. No one is getting hurt.

---

[160] 2 Corinthians 11:14 ESV

- What's one little lie at work, if you can make more money for your family?
- If you can get a new car, house, the latest gadget, or a better job, *then* you will be happy.
- So what if you if you have to make a few necessary compromises, so long as it will open doors for you to gain influence and prestige.
- If you are an overall good person, God will accept you.
- The reason you are suffering is because God is disappointed in you.

All of these are subtle lies from the enemy designed to cut us off from the One who is able to save us, fulfill us, and bring the most joy into our lives. Satan's promise is that all you need is here in this life. Your possessions, your accomplishments, the people you surround yourself with, your career, and yes, even your reputation are of utmost importance. But this stands as a stark contrast to the rhetorical question posed by Jesus: "For what does it profit a man to gain the whole world and forfeit his soul?"[161]

Next, Satan seeks to steal God's plan for your life. Paul's letter to the Ephesians tells us that the Christian is God's workmanship, and we are created in Christ Jesus for good works, which God planned out beforehand.[162] God has given every Christian a work to do. We are to be salt and light in a corrupt and dark world. We are to serve others in the name of Jesus. We are called to proclaim the Good News of God's salvation. Christian brothers and sisters are to encourage one another, pray for one another, strengthen one another, walk alongside one another in the difficulties of life, and enjoy life together. In doing so, we model God's consistent and persistent love towards us. Satan intends to distract us from that work. He does this by making the temporary things of this life

---

[161] Mark 8:36 ESV
[162] Ephesians 2:10

seem urgent and important. He uses our selfish, fleshly desires to steer us away from serving others and entering into a real relationship both with God and our fellow man.

Finally, Satan wants to destroy God's work in us. Philippians tells us, "He who has begun a good work in you will complete it until the day of Jesus Christ."[163] Like any good parent, our Heavenly Father, through His Word, the guidance of His Church, and the circumstances of life, works in us to forge the image of His Son, Jesus. As we press into Him and allow Him to become a very real presence of our lives we find ourselves transformed, made new. Satan despises this because it was his pride and his desire to be like God that led to his downfall. How ironic that God takes the humble and creates in them His own likeness!

Overcoming Temptation

If we are to overcome temptation, we are to first *follow* hard after God and His purposes. We do this in two ways. First, we seek God through His Word. The Psalmist wrote, "Your word have I hidden in my heart, that I might not sin against you."[164] God's Word contains God's person, His purposes, and His promises. His Word gives us wisdom and direction. That is why Jesus was successful in resisting temptation during his time in the desert.[165] When Satan tempted Jesus with lies, Jesus responded with the truth of God's Word.

Following hard after God also means that we remain in consistent fellowship with him through prayer and private worship. Having a conscious awareness of His presence is a strong deterrent to sin. We all know that as children, the closer we were to our parents, the more likely we were to obey and the further

---

[163] Philippians 1:6
[164] Psalm 119:111
[165] Matthew 4:1-11

away, the more likely we were to disobey. In addition, His real presence gives us strength. James backs this up when he writes, "Submit to God. Resist the devil and he will flee from you. Draw near to God and He will draw near to you."[166] It was when David lost sight of God and God's purposes that he opened himself up to temptation.

Next, we are to *flee* temptation. I know this sounds overly simplistic but this is an effective way to win the battle against sin. Paul tells young Timothy to flee youthful lust.[167] He doesn't tell him to build up his spiritual strength, he doesn't tell him to yell at the devil, he doesn't even tell him to pray, even though we should maintain an attitude of prayer. He says, "Flee!" David lingered as he watched Bathsheba from his rooftop. On the other hand, Joseph ran when Potiphar's wife attempted to seduce him. We must take great pains to guard our hearts and keep ourselves from compromising situations. Don't watch that movie, be careful who you are alone with, find a way to safely use the internet, don't go clubbing, don't get involved in that conversation, and so on.

Finally, we must *fight*. Peter tell us to be "sober" and "vigilant" because our adversary is like a lion seeking whom he may devour.[168] He commands, "Resist him." Paul tells us to "put on the whole armor of God."[169] We are the "Church militant" which means as long as we inhabit this earth, we are engaged in warfare. Our battle is fought on our knees as we humble ourselves before God. It is fought as we do good to those who hate us. It is fought by our unflinching obedience to God's Word in a rebellious world. It is fought as we deny ourselves in order to serve others. It is fought as we seek to be transformed by renewing our minds. It is fought in the secret place of prayer as we confess our sins, tear down strongholds, intercede for others, and worship God in spirit and in truth.

---

[166] James 4:7-8
[167] 2 Timothy 2:22
[168] 1 Peter 5:8
[169] Ephesians 6:11

When We Fall

One last note. It is inevitable that we will falter in our Christian walk. As the Accuser, Satan, will make every attempt to condemn us and cause us to question our faith and our relationship with God. This leads to feelings of inadequacy and may even cause us to walk away from church, thinking we will never be able to measure up. Recognize condemnation for what it is: a lie of the enemy. While condemnation drives us from God and His Church, conviction draws us back to God. When we sin, God is not done with us, but as a loving Father reaches out to us. That is why John writes, "If we confess our sins, He is faithful and just to forgive us our sin and cleanse us from all unrighteousness."[170]

Our response to sin is sincere, ongoing repentance. Martin Luther made this clear when he posted his *95 Theses* preceded by a declaration that *all* the Christian's life is one of repentance. David was far from a perfect man but he was a repentant man. His repentance was not merely saying, "I'm sorry," but an inward agony coupled within a passionate desire to change. This is one of the marks of true saving faith. As we persist in our repentance, we acknowledge God's power to save and sustain us in our fight against sin.

---

[170] 1 John 1:9

9

The Church

And on this rock I will build my church, and the gates of Hades shall not prevail against it. —Matthew 16:18b

The followers of Jesus were making a name for themselves in the city of Jerusalem. Peter preached powerfully on the Day of Pentecost seeing three thousand baptized and added to the church. Those followers would then gather on a regular basis to learn from the apostles and to worship and fellowship with one another. Peter and John even healed a man who had never walked before, and wouldn't you know, they were thrown in jail for that good deed. They then boldly defied the command from the Sanhedrin not to preach in the name of Jesus anymore, which would eventually lead to more jail time and a beating. The love of these followers was tangible as they sacrificed to meet each other's needs and serve one another. God was feared, miracles were abundant, prisons couldn't hold these followers of the Way, and punishment only seemed to fuel their passion.

One would think this new movement was not only an unstoppable force but an ideal society filled near perfect people. However, it wasn't long before a major conflict arose. The first followers of Jesus were mostly Jews. Some were homegrown Jews from Judea that held tightly to Jewish culture and customs while others were Hellenistic Jews that either came from outside the region or adopted aspects of the Greek culture. The conflict originated when the widows of the Hellenistic Jews were neglected in the daily distribution of food.

As the disciples contemplated a solution, they recognized that their primary responsibility was to preach and teach the Word of God, and that was the foundation upon which this new movement was built. However, the neglect of one group of widows over another was unacceptable. So, the disciples sought out seven men with good reputations and full of the Holy Spirit to oversee this vital ministry. Each of these men were Hellenists themselves and their service to the church was not limited to serving tables. In fact, one of the men, Stephen, would become the church's first martyr: stoned to death as he was preaching the Gospel.

Eight years after Pentecost, Peter was taking a nap when he had a dream of a great sheet filled with all kinds of unclean animals. A voice said to him, "Get up, Peter. Kill and eat."[171] Peter responded as any good Jew would, "That will never happen." He was sharply rebuked, "What God has made clean, do not call common." Peter had no idea what the dream meant until a few men showed up at the door asking for him. They wanted him to come with them to the home of a Roman centurion named Cornelius. As a good Jew, Peter would never be caught dead in a Gentile home, but his dream was beginning to make sense. The next day Peter went to Cornelius's home where he preached the Gospel while personally coming to the conclusion, "God has shown me that I should not call any man common...But in every nation anyone who fears him and does what is right is acceptable to him."[172] That day everyone in Cornelius's home was saved.

Around twelve years after Peter's visit to the centurion's home many of the church leaders in Jerusalem, including James (Jesus's

---

[171] Acts 10:33 NIV
[172] Acts 10:28 & 35 ESV

brother), met with Paul and Barnabas. There was a major topic up for debate: Must a Gentile must be circumcised and keep the law in order to be saved? It may seem silly in our culture, but the Bible says, "Paul and Barnabas had no small dissension and dispute with them..."[173] In other words, they had a verbal brawl with some of the Jerusalem church leaders.

In that meeting both Peter and Paul made a passionate defense for the Gentiles to be accepted into the Church solely by their profession of faith in Jesus Christ. Peter went so far as to point out the absurdity of their demands saying,

> Why are you putting God to the test by placing a yoke on the neck of the disciples that neither our fathers nor we have been able to bear? But we believe that we will be saved through the grace of the Lord Jesus, just as they will.[174]

The next line is very telling, "And all the assembly fell silent."[175] Paul and Barnabas then tell of how they've experienced miracles and wonders as they preached to the Gentiles. At the core of this counsel was the realization that God was creating for Himself a people who refused to be separated by nationality, ethnicity, tradition, or even their past. Rather, they find their identity in Jesus Christ.

Many romanticize the early church, thinking it was pure and absent of conflict, but that is far from the truth. The merging of imperfect people from different backgrounds and cultures will always bring tension and conflict. So, no, we don't see a perfect church in the pages of Acts, but what we do see is a group of people going out of their way to love one another, serve one another, accept one another, be patient with one another,

---

[173] Acts 15:2 KJV
[174] Acts 15:10-11 ESV
[175] Ibid, v. 15

challenge one another, encourage one another, and yes, even put up with and correct one another. Most importantly, they were resolutely devoted to the mission of preaching the Gospel and making disciples of *all* nations.

What is the Church?

Through the ages, the Church has been misunderstood, mischaracterized, maligned, and heavily persecuted. Early on it was thought by the Roman Empire the church practiced cannibalism, because they partook of the *body* and *blood* of Jesus in communion. It was also said that its members practiced incest since they called one another brother or sister. Eventually, the Roman Empire systematically persecuted and slaughtered many Christians because of their refusal to partake in the emperor cult.

On the flipside, during the Middle Ages, the hierarchical Roman Catholic Church saw itself as the only true church and at times, dealt severely with anyone who questioned its doctrine or authority. Centralizing its power in Rome, it wielded its seeming authority over the sacred attempting to establish influence over the laity and forge an ideal society that encompassed both the sacred and the secular. In addition, many of its leaders were more consumed by the quest for temporal power than the proclamation of the Gospel. This resulted in a corrupt institution that was marked by extravagance and vice. The Church became extraordinarily wealthy while many of its leaders indulged in sexual promiscuity and exploitation. Some feel it was the church's exploitation in the selling of indulgences (a way to reduce punishment for sin in the afterlife) that led to the Reformation.

Today there are a wide range of opinions concerning the Church. Some see it as a force of cultural oppression imposing its morality and outdated values on others. They describe it as judgmental or "holier than thou." Others believe it's an organization in which people are simply told what to believe and how to live. At the same time, many in the Church see themselves as an ignored and oppressed minority. Even those in the church may not fully understand what the church is, thinking it is just a place they go on Sunday or it's an organization that does good things in the community.

So, what is the Church? The world "church" comes from the Greek term, *Ekklesia*, which means *a called out assembly*. Thus, a church is not a building or an organization but a people called out of the world for a specific purpose. The Church as a whole is sometimes called the *Church Universal* and includes every believer throughout history and today. There is also the local church, which includes everything from your old white country church to the church that meets in the school auditorium to the megachurch seen on television. In any event, the Church is also the dwelling place of God; for where God's people are, He is in their midst.

Simply put, *the Church is God's people seeking to fulfill God's mission.* Acts 2:42–47 shows what this actually looks like, "And they continued steadfastly in the apostles' doctrine and fellowship, in the breaking of bread, and in prayers." As the narrative in *Acts* progresses, we see the Gospel spread from Jerusalem to Rome as these same people obey the command of Jesus to make disciples.

The People of God

The people of God are those who have been saved and regenerated by the Holy Spirit through faith in Christ. They are characterized by changed hearts and lives, a passion to please God, and continued spiritual growth. That doesn't mean everyone in church is truly saved. St. Augustine talked about the visible and invisible church. The visible church, being the church as people see it, maybe gathered on a Sunday morning. The invisible Church is the Church as God sees it. It is His people who are growing up as wheat among the tares.[176] That being said, it needs to be understood that within a church body, you will have both true Christians and those who falsely claim the name of Jesus.

God's people are also organized under Godly leadership and the Word of God. In 1&2 Timothy & Titus Paul paints a picture of what these leaders should look like. Overall, they should be honorable, moral, hardworking, and hospitable men who love their families well. In addition, they are to be humble and an example to all other believers.

Of upmost importance, these men should be well versed in the Word of God and make teaching it their primary responsibility to the church. The godly church leader takes the Bible seriously and seeks to preach and teach it without compromise. Likewise, true Christians are people of the book who submit themselves to the Bible making it the final authority in matters of faith and life. It was Martin Luther's view that "anywhere you hear or see the [the Word of God] preached, believed, confessed, and acted upon, do not doubt that the true *ecclesia sancta catholica*, a 'holy Christian people' must be there."[177]

The church is also a community that embodies real fellowship or *kiononia* in the Greek. This is the type of fellowship that involves close mutual relationships where people share things in common and remain involved in each other's lives. They walk through life together. They share burdens, they weep with together, rejoice together, pray for one another, encourage each other, spur one another to good works, confess their faults to each other, humbly correct and restore each another, and are patient with one another. This is authentic community. Unfortunately, what is usually seen in churches are people pretending everything is just glorious while hiding their struggles and sins.

In his book, *Church Awakening*, Charles Swindoll uses 2

---

[176] Matthew 13:24–30

[177] Alister McGrath, *Christian Theology: An Introduction*, 481.

Timothy to highlight what he calls "timeless characteristics of a contagious ministry." These characteristics show what ferociously devoted Christian community looks like. They are as follows: a place for grace, a place for mentoring, a place for hardship...and fellowship, and a place of selfless endurance.[178] The church is a place where we are allowed to make mistakes and find strength to change and improve. It is also where we find godly examples and others who know our pain.

Finally, the people of God are characterized by passionate worship and sincere prayer. This occurs both privately and corporately. Following the pattern of Scripture, Christians believe that it is vital to gather together weekly for worship and the writer of Hebrews leaves no wiggle room for those who say church attendance isn't that important. He writes, "Let us think of ways to motivate one another to acts of love and good works. And let us not neglect our meeting together, as some people do, but encourage one another."[179] It is in corporate worship where the Christian draws strength and finds guidance in a world that is determined to erase their distinction and influence.

In corporate worship, people exalt God through song, the lifting of hands, tears, quiet contemplation, bended knee, shouts of victory, and even cries of desperation. Corporate worship should also include regular *communion*, which reminds Christians of the sacrificial death of Jesus on their behalf, and *baptism*, which represents the believer's death in Christ and being raised as a new creation.

Privately, Christian people should spend ample time in worship and prayer. Private worship may include singing aloud, wonder and amazement at the creation and/or God's grace in one's life, physically prostrating one's self in adoration of God, writing

---

[178] Charles Swindoll, *Church Awakening* (New York, NY: FaithWords 2010), 82-107.
[179] Hebrews 10:24–25 NLT

down your thoughts, creating a piece of art, and for some, it may even include a charismatic prayer language. However, we must not limit worship to a single act but know that our lives, as a whole, are an act of worship, an offering to God.

I can remember my grandfather, who certainly had no singing voice, singing old hymns while he mowed the grass or did carpentry work. I've walked in on a group of ladies one day at the church laying in the floor crying and speaking in tongues as they embraced one another. My mother would wake up at night and walk around the house quietly worshiping. When my great aunt was dying, I remember my uncle, who was around eighty-three or so at the time, walked up to the altar at church to pray. His weak knees shook as he slowly bowed, he then placed his head in his palm and wept. I thought he was upset and he was, but speaking to him later, I realized he was also worshiping. Serving those around you, striving to live a holy life, comforting the downtrodden, and loving one's enemies are also acts of worship.

The Mission of God

The Church exists for the glory of God alone and nothing brings God more glory than the proclamation of the salvation He has provided in Jesus Christ. Every effective organization has a mission, a reason they exist. When Jesus ascended to Heaven, he gave His disciples a mission: "Go therefore and make disciples of all nations, baptizing them in the name of the Father and of the Son and of the Holy Spirit, teaching them to observe all things that I have commanded you."[180]

In our culture many of those who are saved today will be saved as a direct result of a personal relationship they have with a Christian relative or friend. In other words, people will more likely get saved in someone's living room than at a church altar.

---

[180] *Matthew* 28:19–20a

When Jesus told his disciples to "Go therefore" the phrase literally means, "As you are going." As we live our daily lives, we, as the Church, are to serve others, make ourselves available, and most importantly, look for opportunities to preach the Gospel.

Jesus said that he was sending His people into the world just as the Father had sent Him. Many feel the proclamation of the Gospel is something left up to preachers, pastors, or evangelists but this is a command to every Christian.

As God took on human flesh in the person of Christ, he entered man's world and men's lives. He learned their language, took on their frailties and weaknesses, identified with their suffering, shared in their joys and pains... He met people where they were. He "came down" so to speak. He reached out to the hurting, unleashed His righteous anger on the corrupt, confronted oppressors, sympathized with the weak, played with children, and even experienced the pain of betrayal.

In the same fashion, we, too, must identify with those to whom we seek to minister. We cannot stand aloft demanding that the lost come up to our standards as if we have the Christian life mastered. Rather, the Gospel will most readily be received as we humble ourselves to relate to and serve those around us. This includes being honest about our own failures, struggles, and shortcomings and our desire to correct those things with God's help. We, as Christians, should be people who care and people who are real because, *those outside the church will initially be reached relationally by authentic Christians.*

In the eyes of a rebellious and skeptical world, our sincere love and authenticity will give power to our message. Our prayers, our concern, our kindness, our empathy, our patience, our endurance, our faithfulness, our steadfastness, our honesty, and our display of love will never convert a person but prepares the heart to receive the Gospel. As we humbly serve those outside the church, we then look for the opportunity to "preach" the Gospel because it is the Gospel that saves.

In addition to the proclamation of the Gospel, I think it is interesting that Jesus's command is to make "disciples" not just converts. The church is the place where the Christian should be planted, nourished, and grown in such a way as to bear fruit. Every new Christian should find a good church where God's word is preached and worship is sincere and commit themselves to that body of believers. Every church should seek to create such an atmosphere where Christians can grow and mature.

Final Thoughts on the Church

It is certainly difficult for people in our day to trust others with their deepest needs, thoughts, hopes, and desires. This is where the struggle lies. We're a people who are known only on the surface, a people who rarely open ourselves up for deep examination, a people who are more interested in communicating through the internet than face to face. We present ourselves one way on social media while the reality of our lives is something completely different. However, the church calls us to lower our guard and draw near to people in authentic fellowship. This will not be easy, but it is the most beneficial thing to our soul. It requires that we let down our defenses and be accountable to others. It means that we let others speak truth into our lives, give us an objective view of ourselves, and even rub us the wrong way. Don't let Satan take from you the intimate fellowship the church offers, press in, become vulnerable, seek growth, and desire change. Read what the Prince of Preachers, Charles Spurgeon, wrote about the church,

> Give yourself to the Church. You that are members of the Church have not found it perfect and I hope that you feel almost glad that you have not.... Still, imperfect as it is, it is the dearest place on

earth to us… All who have first given themselves to the Lord, should, as speedily as possible, also give themselves to the Lord's people… the Church is faulty, but that is no excuse for your not joining it, if you are the Lord's. Nor need your own faults keep you back, for the Church is not an institution for perfect people, but a sanctuary for sinners saved by Grace, who, though they are saved, are still sinners and need all the help they can derive from the sympathy and guidance of their fellow Believers. The Church is the nursery for God's weak children where they are nourished and grow strong. It is the fold for Christ's sheep— the home for Christ's family.[181]

Spurgeon's point is clear: Let nothing keep you from committing yourself to a good church so that you may grow up within it.

---

[181] Charles Spurgeon, *The Best Devotion*, a sermon preached in the Metropolitan Tabernacle in England in 1891.

10

Your Place in the Body

*For as we have many members in one body, but all the
members do not have the same function...* —Romans 12:4

In the middle of the first century, Corinth was the most important city in Greece and was, for the Roman Empire, a center of commerce and culture. As a major crossroads for sea traffic, it was also a center of religious and moral corruption. Prostitution was a major enterprise, drunkenness was common, and much like Las Vegas, pleasure seekers from all over the empire came to indulge their baser desires. In fact, there was a term in the day, *Korinthiazomai*, which was a synonym for debauchery and prostitution. In addition, Corinth was a hotbed for many mystery cults, which were underground religions that claimed secret knowledge and were known for their mysterious rituals.

It was into this ruckus environment that Paul and his friends, Aquila and Priscilla, brought the Gospel. As usual, Paul started in the synagogue where the Bible says he "persuaded" both Jews and Greeks. From that small start, a church would be planted. Paul and his friends would remain there for a year and a half to steady the church in its growth, then Paul was off to Ephesus.

It wasn't long, though, before Paul began getting some disturbing reports. The church had allowed this city of corruption to corrupt it. First: sexual immorality. Some guy was sleeping with his stepmother while others were looking for an easy way out of their marriage. Second: idolatry. Many in the church were openly participating in pagan religious rites.

However, the most disturbing stories in Paul's mind involved the palpable division that existed within the church. It was the first issue he addressed in his letter as he passionately writes,

> Now I plead with you, brethren, by the name of our Lord Jesus Christ, that you all speak the same thing, and that there be no divisions among you, but that you be perfectly joined together in the same mind and in the same judgement.[182]

Paul knew that a house divided against itself would fall, so he begs the Corinthians to mend their fractured congregation. The word he uses, "joined," is a medical term for the setting of a bone. Paul saw deep fractures in this body of believers that would never heal unless serious efforts were made to set things right.

This was a church divided in every way. They were divided along socioeconomic lines with some members thinking themselves to be more important than others. This division was so severe that even in the Lord's Supper, the rich were bringing their own food to consume and getting drunk while some of the poorer church members went home hungry. These people even divided themselves up into groups based upon prominent personalities. Paul sharply rebukes them for this stating, "For when one says, 'I am of Paul,' and another, 'I am of Apollos,' are you not carnal?"[183] He goes on to say, "Who is Paul, and who is Apollos, but servants?"

This spirit of division even bled over into the gifts, callings,

---

[182] 1 Corinthians 1:10
[183] 1 Corinthians 3:4

and administrations of the church itself. There were some with more visible gifts and positions who felt themselves above those whose gifts with behind the scenes gifts, and this led to extreme arrogance. In addition, those who were more well off and those with more prominent positions in the church became self-centered, demanding their way and their rights. Paul writes extensively teaching them their wealth and their prominent gifts do not necessarily put them in charge but should humble them and cause them to see themselves as servants rather than masters.

Just like the church at Corinth, every church struggles to maintain unity, and within every church there are sincere Christians struggling to find their place in the Body of Christ. Satan knows if he can divide a church, that church ceases to be effective. If people become brash and self-centered, the church becomes a tool to fulfill their own personal agenda as opposed to God's. On the other hand, if some feel as if their contribution is insignificant or unimportant, they may never fulfill their God-given purpose. Finally, if people fail to realize that the church's battle is not against flesh and blood but against the "rulers of darkness," then they will spend time fighting amongst themselves, defending their opinions, positions, and programs while seeking to discredit their opponent.

Unity

Division within a church is not limited to Corinth. In our day, there are many lines of division: the style of music, a liturgical or a less formal service, Calvinism vs. Arminianism, the continuation of Spiritual gifts, how the church is decorated, small groups or Sunday school, how and when a believer is baptized, and like the Corinthians, we even divide ourselves based upon prominent preachers or teachers. As we move forward in this chapter, we need to keep the following in mind: *Above all else a local church should strive to maintain the unity of the Spirit centered around the proclamation of the Gospel, the maturity of God's people, and a sound Biblical doctrine.* Outside those things, everything else is secondary.

That doesn't mean that these other things aren't important and shouldn't be taken into consideration as one chooses a church. That is what makes Christianity unique. There are numerous churches all over the world that worship in countless different ways yet hold to a core set of beliefs and principles. In the same town, there may be a Presbyterian church that is liturgical and Calvinistic in its doctrine and a Pentecostal church that is more free and Arminian, yet both strive to fulfill Jesus's command to preach the Gospel and make disciples, and both teach the Bible. Every person needs to find a church in which they see God worshiped in spirit and in truth and where the Bible is taught without compromise, and then commit themselves to the people of God in that church. In doing so, they find their place in that body of believers and seek to build it up for God's glory.

With that said, there also needs to be an understanding that everyone will not always agree on ministry methods nor will they likely agree with every single thing taught from the pulpit. Believers need to know what things to hold loosely and what things hold tightly. Aside from the mission of the Church to make disciples of Jesus and some of the core doctrines mentioned in this book, most everything else should be held to loosely. In other words, there are things that believers can debate over, but they should not divide over them. Below you will see a few examples of closed-handed issues (things to ferociously defend) and open-handed issues (things to debate but not divide over):

Closed-handed Issues	Open-handed Issues
The person and work of Jesus	The nuances of sanctification
The need for salvation in Christ alone	The question of losing one's salvation
The inspiration and authority of the Bible	The continuation of Spiritual gifts
The fallen nature of man	Style of worship music
The Trinity	Ministry methodology
The command evangelize	Eschatology

Not only must there be unity within the body but also unity *as* the body. Ephesians chapter two tells us that the members of the church have been "fitted together." While Ephesians uses the metaphor of a building, 1 Corinthians uses the metaphor of a human body and states, "The body is one and has many members, but all the members of that one body, being many, are one body, so also is Christ."[184] Paul is driving home a clear point with both of these metaphors: *Even though the church is made up of many different members with different functions, they are all a part of the same body working toward the same goal.*

God has placed every member of the church there for a specific purpose, and just like the human body, every part is intimately connected and dependent upon the other parts of the body. So, Paul writes, "The eye cannot say to the hand, 'I have no need you.'"[185] The reality is that every part of the body plays a vital role. In fact, Paul goes so far as to state that those members who many think are "less honorable" are actually some of the most vital members within the body. This is the people who stay to clean up after church dinner, the woman who does the books for church and charges nothing, the Sunday school teacher who is faithful to his/her one student, the young guy who encourages

---

[184] 1 Corinthians 12:12
[185] Ibid, v. 21

the pastor by showing sincere appreciation, the elder church lady who fights epic battles in prayer when no one is watching, and the widow who sends cards of encouragement to those struggling within her community. Even though these acts of ministry are rarely applauded, it doesn't mean they are not important. These ministries and callings may never be applauded this side of Heaven, but you can rest assured when it's all said and done, these men and women of God will be greatly rewarded.

Leadership

Unity and success are closely tied to leadership. It is amazing how an NFL or college football coach can take a team with a losing record and turn essentially the same team around in just one or two seasons. Those upfront set the tone, and the Church has one that has done that like no other, Jesus Christ. He is the church's source of life and nourishment, the church's supreme example, the object of the church's worship, and it is He who gives direction to the church through its leaders. Ephesians chapter four says,

> But to each one of us grace was given according to the measure of Christ's gift... And He Himself gave some to be apostles, some prophets, some evangelists, and some pastors and teachers, for the equipping of the saints for the work of ministry, for the edifying of the body of Christ, till we all come to the unity of the faith and the knowledge of the Son of God, to a perfect man, to the measure of the stature of the fullness of Christ.[186]

These leaders carry the responsibility of nurturing and

---

[186] Ephesians 4:7-13

maturing other believers through the teaching of God's Word and their godly example. Ultimately, however, their end goal is to forge Christians who are fruitful in every way. That means they manifest the "fruit of the Spirit" and strive, through proclamation and service, to see souls saved.

The characteristics of these leaders are most prominently laid out in 1&2 Timothy and 1 Peter 5:3. They are as follows (in no certain order):

- A passionate desire for the work
- A mature faith
- Self-control
- A knowledge of the Word the ability to teach it
- Gentleness
- Generosity

- Good husbands and fathers
- Good employees
- Good managers of their homes
- Endurance
- Reliable
- Diligence
- Examples to the church

Gifts & Callings

As I mentioned earlier, there are a few places in the New Testament that speak of the church as a body, and just like a body has different parts with different functions, all of which are vital, the church has different parts with different functions. Every Christian is different and has a specific role to play. Let me get personal here, if you are a Christian, *you* have a role to play in your local church. Your passion should be to discover what that role is and seek, with the aid of the Holy Spirit, to fulfill it.

So, you may ask, what is my gift or calling? There are many who would point you to Romans 12 or 1 Corinthians 12 where Paul provides a list of gifts. This may be a good place to start.

However, I feel that these lists are more representative than comprehensive. In other words, there are things in the church one may be called to do that aren't necessarily on one of these lists, but let's take a look at them. Note that the lists in Romans and 1 Corinthians doesn't match up completely but does overlap quite a bit. In addition, there are the leadership gifts we've already mentioned from *Ephesians* chapter four. Check out the chart below.

More Visible Gifts	"Behind the Scenes" Gifts
Prophecy	Service
Word of Wisdom/ Knowledge	Showing Mercy
Teaching	Giving
Leadership/Administration	Discernment
Healing/Miracles	Faith
Tongues/Interpretation of Tongues	Helps
Apostle	Hospitality
Prophet	Encouragement
Evangelist	Intercession
Pastor/Teacher	

Some teachers and theologians would further categorize these. For example, Apostle, Prophet, Evangelist, and Pastor/Teacher could be called "Foundational Gifts."[187] It is not my purpose to navigate those nuances, I simply want to provide an overview of the different ministries within the church so that you may gage where you might fit within a local body of believers.

---

[187] Bryan Carraway, *Spiritual Gifts: Their Purpose & Power* (Enumclaw, WA: Pleasant Word, 2005), 113.

Remember, however, that these lists may not necessarily be comprehensive. For example, there is nothing on these lists about carpentry or décor, yet there is an obvious need for these gifts within a church.

My father-in-law is a skilled carpenter. I truly believe the Spirit of God anointed/gifted him to aid in the construction and remodeling of our current church building. In addition, he has headed up groups on the mission field to improve homes for the poor and put a roof on a church. Art, music, financial aptitude, and others are all talents and/or gifts that are beneficial to the church as well.

One more thing we ought to consider: If we're not careful it is our tendency to think the only holy or sacred things we do are directly connected to the church. So, preaching, leading worship, prayer, and the like are considered the really holy and important callings or activities. Nothing could be further from the truth. ALL of life is sacred and our gifts, talents, and callings are to be employed both inside and outside the church for the glory of God.

Discovering Your Calling

As a part of the body, it is essential that you understand that you have a vital role to play. *We must all strive to discover what that role is because when we do our part, the whole body benefits. However, when we play the slacker, the whole body suffers.*

Discovering your place in the Body of Christ begins with first discovering the heart of God. We must first seek His face before we seek His gifts. As we draw near to God, we find our hearts changed, our selfish ambitions challenged, our motivations purified, and our desires rectified. Ultimately, we are filled with His love for His people. Jesus connected our relationship with God to our relationship with others when He stated the greatest commandment was to, "Love the Lord your God with all your soul and with all your mind and with all your strength. The second is this: Love your neighbor as yourself. There is no greater commandment than these."[188] In the middle of his instruction on spiritual gifts, Paul writes, "Pursue love." Only when we are motivated by our love for God and our love for others will our gifts and service bring forth abundant fruit.

Second, we must become sensitive to the needs of others. It's easy to detach ourselves from the rest of humanity and see their difficulties and struggles as an inconvenience, but Christ calls us to engage with the hurting, to bear the burdens of others, and share in their difficulties and sorrows. Many of Jesus's miracles in the Gospels were preceded by Him being "moved with compassion." The challenge for us then, is to allow the needs of others to motivate us as our own needs would.

Third, in order to discover your gift or calling you must be faithful in the "small things." *The Message* version of Luke 10:16 asks,

> If you're honest in small things, you'll be honest in big things; If you're a crook in small things, you'll be a crook in big things. If you're not honest in small jobs, who will put you in charge of the store?

Ecclesiastes 9:10 says, "Whatever your hand finds to do, do it with all your might." When I took my first job as a child, my mom told me, "Don't stand around, look for something to do... no matter how small it seems." Look for opportunities to serve others. Never be too good for a job. It's so disappointing to see a young man or woman called into the ministry suddenly feel like he or she is above taking out the trash or staying to help clean up after a church dinner. Jesus showed what leadership was when he

---

[188] Mark 12:30-31 NIV

girded Himself with a towel and served the disciples He created by washing their feet.

Finally, let God bring promotion. In his address on love Paul says, "[Love] does not demand its own way."[189] The church is no place to play politics or climb the proverbial ladder. "*God* has put each part where he wants it."[190] We must simply be faithful in that which has been given to us and patient, allowing God to place us where He wants us and when He wants us there. As the One who sees the end from the beginning He is best suited to do this. Imagine the difficulty for Joseph as a slave and a prisoner who knew deep down he was destined to rule in some way! Yet, not one time in Scripture do we see him playing politics or trying to make a name for himself. His waiting was not a passive waiting. Rather, he was faithful, hardworking, and patient, trusting God would bring promotion.

It is essential that every Christian marry themselves to a local body of believers because in order to love the Church for which Christ died, one must be a part of a visible church. You can't love at a distance, and you can't use the excuse that the church is filled with hypocrites so as to avoid commitment or disappointment. Every church is filled with flawed people, and even though you may have it altogether, like Jesus why not condescend to involve yourself in the lives of these helpless, imperfect mortals? All joking aside, God has given every Christian something to offer the body: a gift, a talent, a calling, or a seemingly insignificant service. Rather than be a people who demand our rights, let the church be filled with a people who embrace their God-given responsibilities.

---

189 1 Corinthians 13:4 NLT
190 1 Corinthians 12:18 NLT; *italics mine*

11

Christian Maturity

No prolonged infancies among us, please. We'll not tolerate babes in the woods, small children who are an easy mark for impostors. God wants us to grow up. —Ephesians 4:14 MSG

There was nothing like the feeling of hearing my son say "da-da" for the first time. Then, when he first began to stand on his own, I got so excited knowing it wouldn't long before he would be taking his first steps. In fact, over the next several weeks, I perfected the art of whipping my cell phone out as quickly as possible hoping to catch that moment.

As satisfying as those moments are, I would be disappointed and even worried if my son's development halted at "da-da" and taking a few steps. Thankfully, over the next several months, he would learn new words and went from taking a few wobbly steps to running across the backyard.

Those months were filled with anticipation and anxiety. With every new word, he still had the frustration of not being able to fully express his needs verbally. As he continued to learn to walk, he would fall more times than we could count. In no time, he went from taking a step or two to walking across the room only to fall and hit his head or scrape a knee. On more than one occasion, he'd slip off while our backs were turned, and we would lose him in the house somewhere. One time we found him in the shower playing with shampoo bottles. Another time, we found him trying to get into the dryer. However, one time he got away, and we found him two-thirds the way up our stairs. My wife was horrified and since then we haven't forgotten to put up the safety gate.

With all that said, our expectation is that he will continue to grow and soon he'll be able to express himself in intelligible sentences, and not need a gate to keep him from going up the stairs. As proud as we are to hear the words, "da-da," "mama," or even hear him tell what the rooster says, we still look forward to the day he learns his ABCs, and hopefully earns a college degree. As exciting as it is to see him climb the playground slide by himself, we also look forward to the day he gets his first base hit or comes home with his first paycheck.

Over and over in the New Testament, Paul exhorts his readers to "grow up" in their faith. Salvation was never intended to simply be a ticket out hell but it is redemption, the continual transformation of marred and sinful people into the children of God. For Paul, an immature Christian was the same as a carnal Christian. He says, "I...could not speak to you as to spiritual people but as to carnal, as to babes in Christ."[191] Now, that isn't to say that new believers should become mature in a few weeks or even a few months, but Paul wants the church to understand the danger of remaining babes.

In one of the most controversial passages in the New Testament, the writer of Hebrews states,

> Therefore, let us leave the elementary doctrine of Christ and *go on to maturity*, not laying again a foundation of repentance from dead works and of faith toward God... And this we will do if

---

[191] 1 Corinthians 3:1

God permits. For it is impossible, in the case of those who have once been enlightened, who have tasted the heavenly gift, and have shared in the Holy Spirit, and have tasted the goodness of the word of God and the powers of the age to come, and then have fallen away, to restore them again to repentance…For land that has drunk the rain that often falls on it, and produces a crop useful to those for whose sake it is cultivated, receives a blessing from God. But if it bears thorns and thistles, it is worthless.[192]

Don't get mired in the theological debate posed in this passage.[193] This is a stark warning from the writer of Hebrews, which suggests *the Christian who shows no signs of spiritual maturity may, in fact, be no Christian at all.*

This passage should both scare us and cause us to deeply examine our lives. First, the writer says that people can have spiritual experiences, an understanding of Scripture, and even be used by the Holy Spirit. Jesus even says that many will come in the last days saying, "Lord, Lord, have we not prophesied in Your name, cast out demons in Your name, and done many wonders in Your name?"[194] He doesn't say, "No, you didn't do those things." He says, "I never knew you; depart from Me, you who practice lawlessness."[195] The point of the passage here is that there is more to the Christian life than a spiritual experience, than knowing the Scripture, being part of a church, or even performing good works.

Second, the writer uses the illustration of two pieces of ground which receive rain, yet one produces a useful crop while the other

---

[192] Hebrews 6:1–8 ESV; *italics mine*

[193] This passage is used by some to say that one can lose their salvation: This is part of the classic Calvinism vs. Arminianism debate.

[194] Matthew 7:22

[195] Ibid, v. 23

only thorns and thistles. As the plants begin to sprout, both may seem fruitful, but as they grow, the true nature of the plants are seen. Are you that plant which produces a useful crop or one that merely appears useful?

If you feel the weight of this passage, then the advice in Hebrews 6:12 is actually quite pressing for you: "Do not become sluggish." Fearing you might actually be in danger of "falling away" should move you to action, cause you to strive for maturity. That tension and fear in one's life may actually be evidence of a regenerated heart longing to be continually changed by God.

I seek to instill a fear of hot stoves, running into the road, and putting things into electrical outlets in my children in hopes they will avoid those things. If you don't have at least some apprehension concerning your faith, some desire for growth, then it may be that you need to seriously examine your relationship with God. That doesn't mean you still don't have room for improvement, or that there isn't some sin you still struggle with, or that you have complete peace no matter what. It means you desire to improve and you're seeking spiritual maturity, which takes time, and you are truly concerned about your relationship with God rather than just taking it for granted. So, in the words of Paul, "Examine yourselves as to whether you are in the faith."[196]

Signs of Immaturity

As you examine your life, please know there are many signs of immaturity, but we will limit our list to just three. First, selfishness. From an early age, children have to be taught to share. Even the most innocent baby takes no thought for the fact that their parents need to sleep from time to time. Rather, their appetite, wet diaper, or other immediate needs are made know by furious cries no matter what is going on, where they are, or

---

[196] 2 Corinthians 13:5

what time it may be. As they grow and begin playing with other children, the cry, "mine" will be heard as they begin to fight over toys. Unfortunately, many never grow out of this, even in their adult years.

In the Christian world, this plays itself out when people refuse to sacrifice their comforts or conveniences in order to serve others. The Christian call is one of self-denial and sacrifice. Just like Jesus we are called to set aside our ambitions, desires, and passions in order to meet the needs of those around us.

The second sign of immaturity is a lack of self-control. The inability to control one's appetites, actions, and emotions are prominent in children and teenagers. Proverbs tells us that a person without self-control is like a city with broken down walls.[197] The writer is saying anything can get the better of us. A lack of self-control is manifested in the deeds of the flesh, which are sexual immorality, impurity, lustful pleasures, idolatry, sorcery, hostility, quarreling, jealousy, outbursts of anger, selfish ambition, dissension, division, envy, drunkenness, wild parties, and other sins like these.[198]

Briefly this means rather than being ruled by the Spirit which lives within us, we are enslaved by our own fleshly desires. For example, many cannot control their sexual impulses, which leads to casual sexual encounters despite the danger of STDs or an unwelcomed pregnancy. For many men, this controlling desire may lead to a porn addiction, which could destroy his wife's self-image, undermine her trust, or even end a marriage. The inability to control one's sexual appetites despite these devastating consequences is an obvious sign of immaturity. All that matters is gratifying one's immediate desires or passions at the expense of the future.

Along these same lines is the ability to control one's emotions.

---

[197] Proverbs 25:28
[198] Galatians 5:19–21 NLT

So often it is our emotions that control us. As a teenager, I had a terrible temper. On one occasion, I was cleaning my mom's car and couldn't get the windshield as clean as I felt it should have been. No matter what I did, it kept on streaking. After about fifteen or twenty minutes of wiping I unleashed my frustration by putting my foot through the glass. Looking back, I see how silly it was, but in the moment, my rage had complete control.

The ability to keep one's mouth shut when ridiculed, saying, "no," when every bit of your flesh says, "yes," turning the channel when you know you're about to be tempted, maintaining an even-keel, keeping calm in an intense situation, thinking through moral and practical ramifications of your words and actions are all signs of self-control.

In the church, the Christian ruled by his/her emotions rarely commits to anything long term. As soon as the job gets difficult, they quit or "feel led" in a different direction. The mature Christian presses forward despite their feelings. They do a job even when it is hard, inconvenient, goes unnoticed, or if they don't feel like it anymore.

The Apostle Paul wrote, "I discipline my body and make it my slave."[199] You have a choice: Like a child, you can be dominated by your emotions and fleshly desires, or you can be dominated by the Spirit of God. Remember, you are a slave to whomever you yield yourself to. Don't forfeit your future for the sake of your feelings.

Being easily offended is another sign of immaturity. These are the people that always blame others or their situation for their problems and failures. Statements like, "It's because of what they said or did that I'm in this situation," or "If that had not have happened I would have been successful." They are constantly viewing themselves as the victim and thus feel they have the right to hold a grudge or mistreat others. They refuse to accept responsibility or let mistreatment or misfortune roll off their

---

[199] 1 Corinthians 9:27 NASB

backs. They allow these things to handicap them and use them as an excuse for not fulfilling God's purpose for their lives. In short, they are downright childish.

Marks of Maturity

Now, you can easily flip these preceding marks of immaturity around and see that mature Christians are unselfish, like parents giving up what they want to provide for their children. They are also self-controlled and not easily offended. Again, there are many ways to gage Christian maturity, but we will limit our list to four.

The first sign of Christian maturity is a desire for what is good and right. The growing Christian has a deep passion to please God, to be obedient to His will. Along with spiritual growth, comes the conviction of sin. When mature Christians do wrong or fail to do what is good, it bothers them. This is different than the teenager who apologizes for egging someone's home only because they got caught. Rather, this is the young adult who honestly wants the make their parents proud.

Second, is the desire to embrace responsibility. When writing to the immature Corinthian church Paul makes the statement, "When I became a man, I put away childish things."[200] There comes a time in one's Christian development when you aren't just a consumer (completely dependent on others) but also a producer. Our modern day churches are filled with consumers. These are people who simply show up on Sunday morning thinking they've done God a favor and never commit themselves to the church body nor the work of God through the Church. In addition, there are those who may volunteer but never see anything through to the end. Paul speaks of these kinds of Christians in Ephesians 4,

---

[200] 1 Corinthians 13:11

> I want you to get out there and walk—better yet,
> run! —on the road God called you to travel. I
> don't want you sitting around on your hands...
> And mark that you do this with humility and
> discipline—not in fits and starts, but steadily,
> pouring yourselves out for each other in acts of
> love... No prolonged infancies among us please...
> God wants us to grow up.[201]

Paul is calling on these Christians to be responsible, dependable, and consistent.

The third mark of maturity is a practiced faith. James says that even the demons believe and tremble[202] and then goes on to say that faith without works is dead or useless. Jesus cursed a fig tree which looked fruitful but in reality was fruitless. *Our faith must impact our lives!* Real faith produces good fruit. That is the fruit of Godly character mentioned in Galatians 5:22–26 and most of the book of James. What naturally follows Godly character is good works. Jesus said the world would see our good works and glorify our Father in Heaven.

Some may argue that we're being legalistic insisting that we are saved by faith alone not good works. I would agree. However, I like the statement often attributed to Martin Luther which says, "We are saved by faith alone, but the faith that saves is never alone." Real faith is accompanied by good works that impact the lives of those around us and reflect the nature of our Heavenly Father. Mature faith is more than mere lip service or a mental acknowledgment, it is transformed hearts leading to transformed lives.

Fourth, a mature Christian is a Christian with a sense of purpose. The early church was able to endure and even thrive

---

[201] Ephesians 4 MSG
[202] James 2:19

under persecution, in part, because of their sense of purpose. Paul was driven by his mission to preach the Gospel to the Gentiles. Jesus gave up everything to fulfill His purpose to the point of agonizing over it in the Garden of Gethsemane.

Purpose gives the little things in life meaning. For example, filling sandbags may seem pointless and laborious unless you know a flood is coming. Purpose also gives us motivation when things get difficult or monotonous. Those who live life with no purpose are more likely to quit when things get hard. Our purpose is threefold; We are to enjoy fellowship with God, be continually conformed to the image of Christ, and proclaim the Gospel.

Finally, the mature Christian produces more Christians. This includes both evangelizing the lost and mentoring new Christians. The New Testament is filled with examples of Christians coming alongside one another to provide encouragement and instruction. Barnabas takes Paul under his wing when others were afraid of him. Later on, when Paul wanted to leave Mark behind because he ditched them on their last trip, it was Barnabas who stood up for the young man. Paul and Barnabas would part ways over the issue, but years later, Paul would ask for Mark by name, saying that he was "needful" to him. Barnabas's grace and patience paid off with both Paul and Mark.

It's easy to stand at a distance and criticize others for falling short or failing to live up to the Christian standard. And it is certainly easier to not get involve at all. The difficult work of bearing with and training new believers requires patience and grace. When one sees a weakness in the Body of Christ, rather than criticize it, why not enter a place of prayer and intercession until that weakness is strengthened? Then come alongside that individual, get to know them, earn their trust, speak truth into their lives, and let them learn from your mistakes and their own.

Means of Maturity

So, *how* do we mature as Christians? Let's look briefly at five means of maturity: the nutrition of the Word, the exercise of our faith, the cleansing of our lives, the love of God's people, and our focus as we move forward.

The Bible calls itself bread, milk, honey, solid food, & meat. An appetite for the Word of God is evidence that you are alive spiritually while a loss of appetite is an indication of spiritual sickness. In order to maintain our spiritual health and continue to grow, we must feast on God's Word daily. We can't neglect our spiritual diet, then expect a minister to force feed us once or twice a week and expect to grow.

Also, we can't fill ourselves with the ideas and philosophies of the world and expect it not to have a negative impact on our spiritual growth. No one in their right mind would eat a healthy meal, then include a side of arsenic. That's not to say that we don't have an understanding of how those outside the church think and live or refuse to familiarize ourselves with different religious beliefs. How else would we be able to minister to those people? It's just that we don't *digest* those ways of thinking and believing, so they become part of what shapes our lives.

In addition, we can't feast solely on spiritual junk food, like what makes up much of televangelism, where one is told that if they have enough faith, then wealth and divine health is theirs for the asking. Or, perhaps, we only focus our studies on the aspect of God and His Word that appeal to us personally, rather than struggling with the whole counsel and the whole character of God.

Next, we must exercise our faith regularly. This includes the application God's Word, private prayer, fasting, verbal praise and worship, consistent church attendance, evangelizing the lost, striving the live righteously, and serving and being good to others. All of this includes the ability to put off the old man and put on the new man. It also requires self-discipline and dependence upon

God. However, if we do these things consistently, not in fits and starts or just when the notion strikes, we find we are stoking the fire of the Spirit of God that lives within us and strengthening that inner man whose desire is to please God, enjoy Him, and do what is good and right.

Third, we need to regularly examine our lives and seek that cleansing that comes from God. We are cleansed through the regular practice of repentance. Repentance is more than saying, "I'm sorry" or confessing one's sin. Repentance is a deep sorrow for sin that leads to confession and an impassioned desire to change.

God also uses the furnace of persecution and the difficulties of life to cleanse us. Knowing He uses *all* circumstances for our good, we can look at all the frustrations, struggles, and even the injustices of life with a sense of purpose. God uses *all* of life for our good and His glory. Peter uses the illustration of gold refined in the furnace to show that suffering brings the impurities of our lives to the surface so they can be dealt with in prayer and repentance.

The fourth means of maturity is the love of God's people. Being surrounded by a sincere, authentic Christian community is not just a good idea but a necessity for the Christian. The Christian community in the form of the local church provides us with encouragement, correction, Godly counsel, accountability, an objective voice, inspiration, and instruction. No one who grows up in isolation is as whole and spiritually fit as they should be.

Finally, we grow because of our focus. Hebrews 12:1–2 says, "Let us lay aside every weight, and the sin which so easily ensnares us, and let us run with endurance the race that is set before us, looking unto Jesus, the author and finisher of our faith." It has been said that you become what you behold. Children often become more like their parents, both good and bad, than they realize because the parent is the greatest influence on the character of a child. We must struggle to push past the distractions of this world. We must keep Jesus always before us knowing that as we do so, we are instilled with His character and His power.

FINAL THOUGHTS

There is probably no more intense struggle in human history than what we witness in Gethsemane. In chapter twenty-six of his Gospel, Matthew describes the night before Jesus is to be crucified for the sins of the world. He takes His disciples with Him to the Garden where He usually went to pray. Knowing the excruciating physical and spiritual battle that lay ahead, Jesus throws Himself to the ground in agony and prayer. The Son of God even asks Peter, James, and John to watch and pray with Him. However, the importance and intensity of the moment was evidently lost on them because they ended up falling asleep.

Within a few hours, he would face the cross, and as a man, he balked, likely because he would not only face physical torture, but the forces of evil would come down on Him with relentless vehemence. In addition, and even more tragically, Jesus would face separation from God, His Father, and endure His Divine wrath against sin on behalf of all those who would come to believe in Him. So, it should not shock us to hear Him cry, "O My Father, if it is possible, let this cup pass from Me."[203]

Attempting to find solace and strength, He goes to His friends only to find them asleep. He then retreats back to His place where he prays two more times, "Take this cup from Me." Finally, His struggle ends with the words, "Nevertheless, not my

---

[203] Matthew 26:39

will, but yours be done."[204] Jesus would rise up from that place of prayer strengthened and determined to follow through on the Father's will.

There are five take-a-ways from this event and this book I want to leave with you. First, it's okay to struggle. We have to dispel this notion that Christianity is filled with unflinching saints untouched by the real world, difficult questions, and the circumstances of life. Jesus Christ was no stoic religious figure unphased by difficult decisions and overwhelming challenges. He, too, struggled with the will of God and so will we. In fact, struggling is evidence that one is taking God's will seriously in his/ her lives. John Calvin once wrote, "There are among Christians new Stoics who think it a vice not only to groan and weep, but even to be upset...this cruel philosophy is nothing to us... Our Lord groaned and wept, both for His own and other's difficult circumstances."[205]

Second, we must be honest as we struggle with God. Jesus did not hold back, essentially crying out, "I don't want to do this! If there's any other way, let's take it." It's all too easy to fool ourselves with our Christian faith. Many Christians go through life pretending to be something they are not, even to the point of deceiving themselves. They've cleaned up their lives and started attending church regularly, thinking that's the essence of Christianity. It is not. The Christian faith is an ongoing challenge to be conformed to the image of Christ and that requires us to honestly look at our lives and even our motives. We can't become too easily satisfied with a religion that simply eases our conscience and makes us feel better about ourselves. We must struggle daily to be like Jesus in every action and every attitude. You can't do

---

[204] Luke 22:42

[205] John Calvin. *A Little Book on the Christian Faith* (Orlando, FL: Reformation Trust), pg. 78.

that by thinking you're fine the way you are or justifying actions and attitudes that do not line up with the character of Christ.

In Jesus greatest time of need, he found his friends sleeping, seemingly unmoved by his plight." Third, the struggle can sometimes seem lonely. Notice, however, I said it can *seem* lonely. Often God removes the conscious awareness of His presence. In his book, *The Screwtape Letters*, C.S. Lewis writes,

> Sooner or later He [God] withdraws, if not in fact, at least from their conscious experience... It is during such trough periods, much more than during the peak periods, that it [the Christian] is growing into the sort of creature He wants it to be. Hence the prayers offered in the state of dryness are those which please Him best... He wants them to learn to walk and must therefore take away His hand; and if only the will to walk is really there He is pleased even with their stumbles. Do not be deceived, Wormwood. Our cause is never more in danger, than when a human, no longer desiring, but intending, to do our Enemy's [God's] will, looks round upon a universe from which every trace of Him seems to have vanished, and asks why he has been forsaken, and still obeys.[206]

God is "pleased even with their stumbles." He wants to see us struggling to imitate Him and more fully surrender to His will. Watching us try, even if we fail, is pleasing to Him. He's like a proud parent who sees in their child a determination to succeed or perform while not letting the failures and challenges deter them. Doing God's will when God seems absent or we feel abandoned is real faith and the ultimate goal of our struggle. Loneliness

---

[206] C.S. Lewis, *The Screwtape Letters*, 40.

often helps to forge Godly character or prove it. Moses, David, Elijah, and others often spent extended periods of time alone and certainly times where they felt as if God was a million miles away. I would argue, it was during these times they became the men God intended them to be. Do not despise the seeming times of loneliness.

Forth, though the struggle seems lonely, it can bring us closer to God. As a pastor, I've found it interesting how people are perfectly suited to live their lives barely acknowledging God as long as things are good. His blessings seem to mask His presence and their desperate need for Him. However, many of those same people will frantically call out to God when things go bad. If we will allow, life's challenges, questions about God, and His seeming absence will cause us to call on the Lord and yearn for His involvement in our lives.

Finally, our struggles should always lead to surrender. As much as we fight for our rights, it seems oxymoronic to fight to surrender. But, ultimately, that's what we are called to. Yes, Jesus struggled in the garden, longing for there to be another way. However, he ends his prayer with, "Nevertheless, but as You will."[207] Throughout this book, you have been presented Biblical truths of the Christian faith. Some of which you readily accepted. Others, you may have resisted. Many, you have taken for granted and never deeply considered their impact. Yet, all of them demand the response of surrender. The path to surrender may be longer and more challenging for some than for others but know this, God is pleased with the stumbles, and as long as you keep struggling to know Him and surrender to Him, you are right where He wants you.

---

[207] Matthew 26:39

WORKS CITED

Ambrose. "On the Holy Spirit," *The Nicene and Post-Nicene Fathers*, edited by Phillip Schaff, vol. 7. Grand Rapids, MI: Wm. B. Erdmans Publishing. Christian Ethereal Library. Accessed May 2015. http://www.ccel.org/ccel/schaff/npnf210.i.html.

Battenson, Henry and Chris Maunder, editors. *Documents of the Christian Church*. Oxford: Oxford University Press, 1999.

Bubeck, Mark. *The Adversary*. Chicago, Il: Moody Publishers, 2013.

Calvin, John. *A Little Book on the Christian Faith*. Orlando, FL: Reformation Trust, 2017.

Carraway, Bryan. *Spiritual Gifts: Their Purpose and Power.* Enumclaw, WA: Pleasant Word, 2005.

Chambers, Oswald. *My Upmost for His Highest*. Uhrichsville, Ill: Barbour Books, 1963.

Conyers, A.J. *A Basic Christian Theology*. Nashville, TN: B&H Academic, 1995.

Eggert, Ronald, ed. *Tozer on Leadership*. Camp Hill, PA: Christian Publications, Inc., 2001.

Erhman, Bart. *Bible Contradictions*. Youtube.

Frangipane, Francis. *The Three Battle Grounds*. U.S.A. Advancing Church Publications, 1989.

Hanegraaff, Hank. *The Prayer of Jesus: Secrets to Real intimacy with God*. Nashville, TN: Thomas Nelson Inc., 2001.

Harris, Stephen L., ed. *Understanding the Bible*, 5th ed. Mountain View, CA: Mayfield Publishing Company, 2000.

Kaiser Jr., Walter and Duane Garrett, eds. *NIV, Archaeological Study Bible: An Illustrated Walk Through Biblical History and Culture*. Company, City, Year.

Kendall, R.T. *The Lord's Prayer*. Ada, MI: Chosen Books, 2010.

Lewis, C.S. *Mere Christianity*. New York, NY: Touchstone, 1996.

Lewis, C.S. *The Screwtape Letters*. New York, NY: HarperCollins Publishers, 2001.

Lucado, Max. *God Came Near*. Sisters, OR: Multnomah Publishers Inc., 1986.

McGrath, Alister. *Christian Theology: An Introduction*. Malden, MA: Blackwell Publishing, 2001.

McGrath, Alister. *Christianity's Dangerous Idea: The Protestant Revolution – A History From the Sixteenth Century to the Twenty-First*. New York, NY: HarperOne, 2008.

McGrath, Alister E. *Luther's Theology of the Cross*. Malden, MA: Blackwell Publishing, 1990.

Murray, Andrew. *Experiencing the Holy Spirit*. New Kensington, PA: Whitaker House, 1985.

The Orthodox Presbyterian Church, *The Westminster Shorter Catechism*, https://opc.org/sc.html. Accesses August 2018.

Owen, John. *The Mortification of Sin*. Ross-shire, Scotland: Christian Focus, 2010.

Sproul, R.C. *The Holiness of God*. Kindle ed. Carol Stream, Illinois: Tyndale Publishers, 1985.

Sproul, R.C. *The Mystery of the Holy Spirit*. Carol Stream, Illinois: Tyndale House Publishers Inc., 1990.

Spurgeon, Charles. *The Soul Winner*. Charleston, SC: Bibilobazaar, 2008.

Spurgeon, Charles. *The Best Donation*. www.answersingensis.org, a sermon by C. H. Spurgeon given in the Metropolitan Tabernacle in Newington, England on December 13, 1891. September 2018 https://answersingenesis.org/education/spurgeon-sermons/2234-the-best-donation/.

Swindoll, Charles. *The Church Awakening*. New York, NY: FaithWords, 2010.

Taylor, Justin. *How We Can Know the New Testament Teaches that Jesus is God*. thegospelcoalition.org. (February 8, 2019). August 2019 https://www.thegospelcoalition.org/blogs/justin-taylor/can-know-new-testament-teaches-jesus-god/.

Tozer, A.W. *Tozer: The Mystery of the Holy Spirit*. Alachua, Fl: Bridge Logos, 2007.

Wallace, Daniel B. "New Testament Textual Criticism," *Cross Examined* podcast. (Hosted by Frank Turek, October 18, 2017). June 2018 https://crossexamined.org/podcast_new-testament-textual-criticism-with-dr-daniel-b-wallace/.

Wiersbe, Warren. *Being a Child of God.* Nashville, TN: Thomas Nelson Inc., 1996.

White, R.E.O. "Sin." *Evangelical Dictionary of Theology,* edited by Walter E. Elwell, 2nd ed. Grand Rapids, Michigan: Baker Academic, 2001.

Wright, N.T. *Paul, Arabia, and Elijah.* ntwrightpage.com, pdf. (Originally published in Journal of Biblical Literature vol. 115, 683–692). September 2017 http://ntwrightpage.com/files/2016/05/Wright_Paul_Arabia_Elijah.pdf.

AUTHOR INFORMATION

Sam is the pastor of Pathway Church in Beulaville, NC where he served as youth pastor from 2003 to 2006 while also teaching in the public school system. He has degrees in History and Education from UNCW and a Masters in Theological Studies from Liberty University. Through the years, he and his wife, Brooks, have evangelized, worked in the mission field, pastored, and been honored to identify and mentor numerous young people who have felt the call to ministry. In 2015 Sam returned to Pathway Church where he is privileged to serve the people as their senior pastor alongside his wife and two kids, Kross and Brantley.

Key Note

The challenges of life don't have to derail our Christian walk. Those struggles may be the very thing that God uses to reveal Himself.

www.pastorsamsumner.com
https://www.facebook.com/samuel.sumner.54
www.pathwaychurchnc.com

CPSIA information can be obtained
at www.ICGtesting.com
Printed in the USA
BVHW041523160720
583820BV00011B/436